# WORLD WAR II

## A Photographic History

pil

Publications International, Ltd.

# Buildup to War

n September 18, 1931, a group of Japanese soldiers stationed in the northern Chinese province of Manchuria blew up a few feet of the Japanese-controlled South Manchurian Railway. The incident was used as a pretext to launch an attack by the Kwantung Army, which aimed to occupy the whole of the province and bring its rich resources under Japanese control. This was the start of a decade of escalating violence that would culminate in the German assault on Poland and the start of the Second World War.

The League of Nations did little to protect China from Japanese aggression, and in February 1933 Japan left the League altogether. The world order seemed set to benefit big imperial powers rather than what were called the "have not" powers—those with poor supplies of raw materials, a modest colonial empire, and an alleged imbalance between population and territory.

Japan was only the first of the powers that acted in defiance of the existing order. Italian dictator Benito Mussolini wanted an international revolution by what he called the "proletarian states" against the "plutocratic powers," namely Britain, France, and the United States. From 1932 he hatched plans to conquer the independent African state of Abyssinia (present-day Ethiopia), and in October 1935 Italian forces invaded the kingdom. In December 1937, Italy also left the League.

Adolf Hitler, the Chancellor of Germany, was convinced that Germany was a "have not" power. He adopted the popular idea of *Lebensraum* (living space) as a justification for German territorial expansion and the seizure of new economic resources. He also was convinced that Germany represented a superior culture and was destined to dominate lesser races, namely international Jews. This mix of prejudices and grievances became the basis of German foreign policy.

In November 1936, Germany and Japan signed the Anti-Comintern Pact, which was directed at the international struggle against communism; Mussolini signed it a year later. These three nations wanted to alert the Western powers that they saw themselves as a Fascist bloc increasingly opposed not just to communism, but to Western liberal democracy as well.

The Nazis worked to indoctrinate children in their beliefs. "The Jew is the most dangerous poison mushroom in existence," a mother teaches her son in this 1938 children's book.

SPECIAL 4 A.M. EDITION

GET A DAILY EXPRESS MODEL GLIDER FOR THE CHILDREN

No. 11,970

# Daily Express

WORLD'S LARGEST DAILY SALE

Friday, September 30, 1938      One Penny

BEAR BRAND'S Slimming Sy-metra TRUE FASHIONED Stockings

## The Daily Express declares that Britain will not be involved in a European war this year, or next year either

| Mussolini draws up frontier | # PEACE! | Commission to decide plebiscites |

## AGREEMENT SIGNED AT 12.30 a.m. TODAY

### German troops march in tomorrow: Then occupation gradually until October 10

### FRONTIER GUARANTEED

From SELKIRK PANTON

MUNICH, Friday morning

A PACT of peace was signed in Munich at 12.30 this morning.

ONLY TWENTY-THREE HOURS BEFORE THE WAR ULTIMATUM WAS TO HAVE EXPIRED MR. CHAMBERLAIN, DALADIER, HITLER AND MUSSOLINI REACHED AGREEMENT ON THE CZECHO-SLOVAK PROBLEM.

Under its terms Hitler will march his troops into Czecho-Slovakia tomorrow, but not as far as he meant to under the terms of the German memorandum to Czecho-Slovakia of last week-end.

The official communique says that the heads of the four Governments agree that the evacuation by the Czechs of the Sudeten districts should begin tomorrow and that German troops should begin to occupy Sudetenland progressively from tomorrow, completing the occupation on October 10.

#### WHEN POLAND WILL JOIN

Britain and France undertake to guarantee the new frontiers of Czecho-Slovakia, and Germany and Italy will join in this guarantee when all the questions have been settled.

Poland will join the guarantee when the Polish and Hungarian demands concerning their minorities have been granted. If that has not been done within three months, a new meeting of the four statesmen will be called.

An international commission will decide the territories in which plebiscites are to be held.

Mr. Chamberlain, at 1.36 this morning, came in to the Hotel Regina in Munich and said: "Everything is signed. We are going back today."

He was received by a loud burst of cheering which is still going on as I telephone. The hotel lounge is crowded with both foreigners and Nazis, the Nazis saluting with the Nazi salute and heiling, the foreigners cheering and clapping.

#### PREMIER THANKS CROWD

Mr. Chamberlain thanked the crowd. It is obvious that the Prime Minister feels that all danger to peace is now past.

The plebiscite will be held at the end of November.

Mr. Chamberlain came home, but not to go to bed. At this moment he is continuing his discussions, this time with the Czechs.

Britain, France and Italy have enabled Hitler to keep his word to the German people by allowing him to march into Czecho-Slovakia on October 1.

It is said that as a gesture the German troops who

march in today will wear forage caps instead of steel helmets and will march in quietly.

A German spokesman said that a revised line of demarcation between Germans and Czechs—a new frontier for tomorrow—was drawn up by Mussolini himself.

Mussolini left Munich for Rome at 1.55 a.m., accompanied by Count Ciano. Hitler and Goering accompanied him to the station, and shook him by the hand.

But the German people who have, for weeks, feared war are not celebrating tonight a German victory, but that peace has been preserved. They are thanking the British Prime Minister for that.

General comment in his hotel this morning was: "He is a real peace maker. We have much to thank him for."

### This is what they signed

THIS is the text of the communique:—

"Agreement reached on September 29, 1938, between Germany, the United Kingdom, France and Italy.

Germany, the United Kingdom, France and Italy, taking into consideration the agreement which has been already reached in principle for the cession to Germany of the Sudeten German territory, have agreed on the following terms and conditions governing the said cession and the measures consequent thereupon.

By this agreement they each hold themselves responsible for the steps necessary to secure the fulfilment.

1. The evacuation will begin on October 1.

2. The United Kingdom, France and Italy agree that the evacuation of the territory shall be completed by October 10, without any existing installations having been destroyed and that the Czecho-Slovak Government will be held responsible for carrying out the evacuation without damage to the said installations.

3. Conditions governing the evacuation will be laid down in detail by an international commission composed of representatives of Germany, the

PAGE TWO, COL. ONE

THE PRIME MINISTER MEETS MUSSOLINI AT MUNICH. Picture wired last night; see also Back Page.

"I WHISTLED WITH THE FUEHRER" —Daladier

Weather: cooler (see page 11)

LATEST
CENTRAL 8000

### HE MAY BE SIR NEVILLE

Daily Express Staff Reporter

MR. NEVILLE CHAMBERLAIN is likely to be offered a Knighthood of the Garter—the highest honour the King can bestow—in recognition of his services to the cause of peace.

Mr. Chamberlain's half-brother, Sir Austen, was made a K.G. for his work in bringing about the Locarno Treaty.

#### Premier's wife mobbed

CROWDS of women, rejoicing at the news from Munich, cheered Mrs. Neville Chamberlain for several minutes last night as she left St. Michael's Church, Chester-square, W., where the Archbishop of Canterbury had addressed a broadcast service.

ARE YOU REALLY A GOOD FATHER?

You are fond of your family. You provide them with a good home, education — in fact with everything they need.

But an income payable in the event of your early death is something you have possibly regarded as beyond your means to provide.

Here is a plan which can help you

If you are under 45 you can arrange, by means of the

PRUDENTIAL "Heritage" PLAN

that, should you die within the next 20 years, your family will receive:—

£200 in cash immediately,

£6 a week during the remainder of the 20 years, and

£1,800 cash when the payments cease. If death occurs after 20 years,

£2,000 would be payable immediately.

The Munich Agreement eliminated Czechoslovakia's defensive capability, highlighted the military weakness of Britain and France, and provided all concerned with more time to prepare for war.

5

For Britain, France, and the United States, it was difficult to find ways of containing the sudden crisis. None of the three wanted to risk a major war so soon after the last, but none of them wanted to let the world order slide into chaos. There were powerful pressures against an active foreign policy. The British and French empires were menaced by anticolonial nationalism in India, Indochina, the Middle East, and Africa.

Another issue was the attitude of the two potential economic and military giants of the 1930s, the United States and the USSR. In the United States, the impact of the Great Depression after 1929 encouraged a mood of isolationism. When Franklin D. Roosevelt was elected president in 1932, he promised to heal America first and to avoid any international policies that compromised that priority. Congress adopted the provisional Neutrality Law in 1935, then passed permanent legislation in 1937 designed to prevent the United States from giving aid to any combatant state.

The Soviet Union was an unknown and potentially dangerous power. In the 1930s, the USSR began a program of massive industrialization and rearmament, which made Russia the third largest industrial economy by 1939 and, on paper, the world's biggest military power. Yet Soviet leader Joseph Stalin concentrated on building up the new Soviet system and defeating the remaining domestic "enemies" of the revolution rather than act more forcefully in international affairs. The Soviets did not want war, and hoped to minimize its risks.

In September 1934, the Soviet Union was admitted to the League. However, Britain and France were wary throughout the 1930s of any commitment to the Soviet Union. Although a pact of mutual assistance was signed between France and the USSR in May 1935, it was never turned into a military alliance.

Evidence of Western hesitancy encouraged the revisionist powers to press on. Japan began full-scale war with China in 1937 and conquered much of China's eastern seaboard by 1938. In Europe, Hitler ordered his generals in May 1938 to plan an autumn war against Czechoslovakia. But when German pressure reached a peak in the summer, Britain and France intervened. The result was the Munich Agreement signed on September 30, 1938. War was averted, and Hitler was forced to back down from the destruction of Czech independence.

Unhappy that he had not gone to war with the Czechs, Hitler added Britain and France to his list of potential enemies. But he turned first to the east, annexing a large part of Czechoslovakia in March 1939, before insisting that Lithuania and Poland cede Memel and Danzig and come into the German orbit. Only Poland refused to subordinate itself to Berlin, so Hitler decided to attack that country. In a secret agreement with the Soviet Union, he agreed to partition Eastern Europe on the assumption that he would conquer it all after defeating the Western powers.

On August 31, despite mounting evidence of Western firmness, Hitler ordered the campaign to begin the next day. Heinrich Himmler, his security chief, repeated what Japanese soldiers had done in Manchuria in 1931 by staging a fake act of provocation. In alleged retaliation, German forces advanced on a broad front into Poland on the morning of September 1, 1939.

A political cartoon published in the London magazine *Punch* portrayed a widely held British view of Hitler and Stalin's evil nature.

# World War II Begins

On September 1, 1939, the Germans invade Poland with a three-front *Blitzkrieg*–a swift attack with combined air and mobile land forces. They attack the Polish army with an overwhelming force of 1.5 million troops backed by tactical aircraft in the sky and mobile armor on the ground.

At dawn on September 1, 1939, the *Wehrmacht's* armored spearhead swept into Poland. In a foretaste of *Blitzkriegs* to come, armor, infantry, and artillery fought as a closely coordinated team, while the *Luftwaffe* rained death from the skies. General von Bock's Army Group North struck into Poland from Pomerania and East Prussia. Simultaneously, General Rundstedt's Army Group South surged northeast from Slovakia and Silesia. Behind the German armored divisions, some 40 infantry divisions stood ready to exploit the panzers' successes. Everywhere, the woefully unprepared Polish forces were shocked by the speed, scale, and ferocity of the German onslaught.

Although Poland had the fifth largest armed forces in Europe, it was unprepared for a modern war of maneuver. In fact, it still included many horse-mounted fighting units (*pictured*). Despite having well-prepared defensive positions, its mobilized divisions were dispersed too widely to prevent a viable defense against a mobile fighting force like the *Wehrmacht*.

A group of Polish Catholic women pray before the crucifix at a church partially destroyed by German bombing.

As commander-in-chief of the Polish forces, Marshal Edward Smigly-Rydz (*pictured, front*) had the all-but-impossible task of countering the German invasion with outdated defense forces. Poland's borders were generally indefensible because of the lack of rivers and mountains, making its demise inevitable.

# Germany's *Luftwaffe* Bombs Warsaw

On September 25, 1939, Warsaw is bombed into utter submission by the German *Luftwaffe*, the most advanced and powerful air force in the world. The city surrenders to the Nazis on the 27th.

The Germans besieged Warsaw, systematically bombing and shelling the city, causing extensive damage and loss of life. The city's own air defenses were overwhelmed by the tempo of the *Luftwaffe* onslaught, while the outclassed Polish air force was effectively neutralized by September 17.

The German capture of Warsaw proved costly for Germans and Poles alike. After more than two weeks of intensive air bombardment and ground combat, characterized by a succession of closely coordinated ground and air assaults and artillery bombardments, the city finally fell on September 27.

Kazimiera Mika, a 10-year-old Polish girl, stoops over the body of her older sister. The elder Mika girl and six other women, desperate for food, had been digging for potatoes in a field in besieged Warsaw when the *Luftwaffe* struck.

An existing international perception that the *Luftwaffe* routinely used the terror bombing of civilians as a deliberate strategy was undoubtedly reinforced by the campaign.

By the end of the four-week campaign in Poland, 50,000 German soldiers were dead, wounded, or missing. Polish losses amounted to some 70,000 soldiers killed and 130,000 wounded. Another 90,000 Polish soldiers escaped to Hungary, Lithuania, Romania, and Latvia.

# Nazis Begin to Consolidate the Jewish Population

The Nazis begin to consolidate the Jewish population in Germany's occupied territories. They send Austrian and Czechoslovakian Jews to Poland. On November 4, Warsaw's Jews are herded into a ghetto.

Soon after the German victory, the SS death squads in Poland began their work of dealing with what the Nazis termed the "Jewish question." These two Polish Jews are about to be murdered once they have completed digging their own graves. Such denigration contributed directly to a victim's dehumanization, and consequently to a perverse legitimization by the Nazis of such atrocities. Of the approximately six million European Jews murdered during the Holocaust, 2.9 million were Polish.

The Germans arrived at Plonsk, Poland, in September 1939, and established a ghetto the following year. During the next two years, as many as 12,000 Jews from Plonsk and the surrounding area passed through the ghetto. It was eventually emptied in November 1942 when its remaining inhabitants were consigned to Auschwitz for extermination.

Kielce, Poland, fell to the Germans on September 4. This was quickly followed by the deliberate persecution of its Jewish community, with expropriations, deportations (*pictured*), fines, hostage-takings, beatings, and killings. A formal ghetto was set up in Kielce in April 1941, and by 1942 it held 27,000 inhabitants. Thereafter, the Kielce Ghetto's Jews were systematically murdered—either in place or via the extermination camps.

# Hitler Invades the Low Countries

Asserting that the Allies are planning to use neutral nations Belgium, Luxembourg, and the Netherlands as a staging area for an attack on Germany, Hitler invades the Low Countries.

German paratroopers who have just taken the "impregnable" Fort Eben-Emael in Belgium relax after their success. In history's first glider-borne assault, nine silent, engineless aircraft landed on the Eben-Emael roof on May 10, 1940. Resistance was over in 30 minutes, and the entire garrison surrendered in 30 hours.

On May 10, 1940, German tanks, troops, and bombers smashed into France and the Low Countries in a *Blitzkrieg*. Belgium, Luxembourg, and the Netherlands fell quickly. Here, a French tank crewman surrenders to German forces.

Belgian civilians hide from German soldiers. During the May 1940 *Blitzkrieg*, planes bombed and killed some 30,000 civilians.

# Churchill Becomes Prime Minister

inston Churchill becomes Britain's prime minister when Neville Chamberlain, who was losing support in Parliament, resigns.

Winston Churchill did more than any other leader to attain Allied victory in World War II. On May 10, 1940, the very day that Hitler unleashed his *Blitzkrieg* against the Low Countries, Churchill succeeded Neville Chamberlain as prime minister. Churchill's stamina, decisive leadership, and ability to inspire helped Britain achieve victory.

First Lord of the Admiralty Winston Churchill congratulates sailors of HMS *Hardy* on April 19, 1940, for distinguishing themselves during the fighting in Norway. Elevated to prime minister in May, Churchill faced a possible German invasion with a drastically weakened military and a Home Guard of boys and old men armed with everything from old rifles to pitchforks.

# The *Luftwaffe* Rains Terror on France

French civilians flee danger and destruction during the aerial bombardment of Dunkirk, France, by the *Luftwaffe*. British Expeditionary Forces Captain Richard Austin wrote: "The whole front was one long continuous line of blazing buildings, a high wall of fire, roaring and darting in tongues of flame, with the smoke pouring upwards and disappearing in the blackness of the sky above the rooftops." Dunkirk was reduced to rubble.

British soldiers wait for rescue on Dunkirk Beach. When the planned evacuation was announced to the British public, a fleet of small boats rushed across the English Channel to help. These "Little Ships" quickly gained legendary status, and the "Spirit of Dunkirk" became a British rallying cry.

Firemen turn their hoses on a Parisian building that has been reduced to smoldering ruin by Nazi bombardment. On June 3, 1940, 200 planes struck airfields, industrial sites, and buildings in Paris. This successful German effort to damage France's economy, reduce its military, and create terror in its population had a devastating psychological effect. To keep government officials at their posts, the French minister of interior had to threaten dire penalties against any who fled.

British and French soldiers leave Cherbourg, France, on British ships bound for Southampton, England. After the successful evacuation at Dunkirk, the British rescued an additional 220,000 Allied troops that had been stranded in France.

Dunkirk evacuees escape by ship. The British evacuees included many highly experienced soldiers who were eager to return to the fight but had lost all of their equipment.

# France Surrenders to Germany

The railway car in which French marshal Ferdinand Foch had dictated terms to Germany in 1918 was dragged out of its storage shed and returned to the same forest clearing near Rethondes. CBS war correspondent William Shirer noted in Hitler's expression "a sort of scornful, inner joy at being present at this great reversal of fate—a reversal he himself had wrought." On June 22, 1940, the Germans dictated armistice terms that left most of France occupied and set up Vichy France in the area that remained.

On June 14, 1940, German troops marched past the *Arc de Triomphe* (*pictured*) and hung swastika flags on the arc, the Eiffel Tower, and other public buildings. Aware that the enemy had blasted through the Maginot Line, many Parisians had already abandoned the city. Defeatism gripped the French nation.

# British Attack French Ships

With the Vichy regime running France, Britain takes measures to prevent the occupying Nazis from controlling the French Navy. The British sink parts of France's fleet in Algeria and commandeer French ships in British ports. The two countries break off diplomatic relations on July 4.

The French battleship *Bretagne* burns in an Algerian port after being hit by British fire on July 3, 1940. A British ultimatum to the French demanded that the French ships either join with the British, sail under control to a British port, sail to a French port in the West Indies and be demilitarized, or be entrusted to the U.S. When no response came in six hours, Churchill gave the order to attack.

Hitler had assumed that Britain would submit once France had collapsed, but when it became clear that Britain would fight on he ordered the invasion plans to be finalized.

# Germany's Blitz Bombing of London Begins

Although the *Luftwaffe* has been attacking Britain since August, on September 7, 1940, Germany turns its attention from British military to civilian targets.

On September 7, 1940, 300 *Luftwaffe* bombers and 600 fighters attacked London in the late afternoon, and a further 180 bombers continued the raid throughout the night. The resulting destruction and fires (*pictured*) were widespread; 430 civilians died and 1,600 were seriously wounded.

During the Blitz, thousands of Londoners slept in Underground (subway) stations. There, they were fairly well protected from the constant hail of bombs that fell upon the capital.

On the night of September 7, only 92 antiaircraft (AA) guns were deployed about London, and the fire-control arrangements failed almost at once. Thus, the *Luftwaffe* enjoyed three nights with virtually no AA fire directed against it. However, by September 11, some 200 AA guns were put in place, together with supporting searchlights, so that a blaze of light and a curtain of fire (*pictured*) greeted the bombers that night.

From September to mid-November 1940, an average of 200 Axis aircraft bombed London on every night but one. Countrywide, from September 1940 to May 1941, the Blitz caused 43,000 civilian deaths and 139,000 serious injuries, as well as laying waste to many residential areas and infrastructure facilities.

# Franklin D. Roosevelt Is Elected to a Third Term as President

After guiding America through the Great Depression in the 1930s, the tremendously popular Franklin Roosevelt is elected to a third term, a break from the presidency's traditional, though not then mandated, two-term limit.

When war broke out in September 1939, Roosevelt's attempts to aid America's allies in Europe were blocked both by Congress and a majority of American citizens committed to the policy of neutrality and isolationism. America's experience in World War I had soured many on the idea of any more "European entanglements," if only because of the great monetary cost. The realities of the Depression had encouraged a shrinking of the American worldview; U.S. concerns, in the minds of many, overrode all others. FDR fought hard to break through this resistance because of a conviction that if the Axis powers were successful in their conquests, the United States would eventually become the only surviving democracy in the world.

Even though Republican lawyer and industrialist Wendell Willkie ran against President Roosevelt in 1940, he was no isolationist. After his loss, Willkie became a strong supporter of Roosevelt's Lend-Lease Act and urged unlimited aid to Britain.

"We cannot escape danger or the fear of danger, by crawling into bed and pulling the covers over our heads."

—PRESIDENT ROOSEVELT, DECEMBER 29, 1940

Convinced that no foreign power could successfully attack a fully prepared America, the America First Committee encouraged maintaining a strong national defense.

FDR appointed Joseph Kennedy ambassador to Britain in 1938. Kennedy expected Britain to be defeated, and some of his speeches even seemed to imply sympathy with Hitler. Forced to resign in November 1940, Kennedy was succeeded by John G. Winant, an advocate of the Lend-Lease program.

# The Sheffield Blitz Takes Place

Sheffield is a key British armaments center that produces everything from bayonets to armor, including crucial components of the Spitfire aircraft. The Sheffield blitz occurs on the nights of December 12 and 15, 1940, when more than 660 people are killed and nearly 80,000 buildings damaged.

In Britain, Air Raid Precautions wardens operated from local posts, with about 10 wardens per square mile in urban areas. They were responsible for blackout enforcement, bomb reporting, working with the emergency services, and acting as the "eyes and ears" of the Civil Defense organization.

The bombs fell on the city center (*pictured*) rather than the steelworks, which remained largely untouched. Though many civilians took cover in shelters, some were killed while sheltering in basements, most tragically in the Marples Hotel.

# The *Luftwaffe* Begins Its Firebombing of British Cities

Citizens inspect a demolished school and damaged houses after a 1940 German bombing raid on Liverpool, England. That year, Liverpool was hit with more than 300 air attacks. In addition to the well-known London Blitz, German bombers struck at industrial cities and ports all over England, Scotland, and Wales. *Luftwaffe* planes flew from Scandinavia to targets in northeastern Great Britain.

The Fairey Swordfish torpedo bomber entered service with the British Royal Navy's Fleet Air Arm in 1936. Although limited by a slow speed of 138 mph and armed with just two machine guns, the carrier-launched biplane had much to offer. It was highly maneuverable, had a range of more than 500 miles, and could carry either a 1,620-pound torpedo or the equivalent weight of bombs, mines, or depth charges.

# Roosevelt Increases Defense Spending to $10.8 Billion for 1942

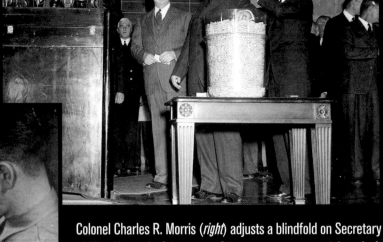

Roosevelt's $10 billion buildup of the military includes a two-ocean navy, as well as the first peacetime conscription in U.S. history. By June 1941, the Army is nearly 1.5 million strong. Yet Roosevelt still insists that the U.S. will not join the fighting, remaining instead the "Arsenal of Democracy."

Colonel Charles R. Morris (*right*) adjusts a blindfold on Secretary of War Henry L. Stimson as Stimson prepares to pick a draft number out of a large bowl. The Selective Service Act of 1940 required every American male citizen or resident alien from age 21 through 35 to register for a draft number.

New American draftees get simultaneous injections from medical officers at Fort Dix, New Jersey. After conscription, all inductees received a smallpox vaccination and an inoculation against typhoid.

An Army paratrooper

# The House of Representatives Passes the Lend-Lease Bill

ongress supports Roosevelt's "Arsenal of Democracy" and passes the Lend-Lease Act, which authorizes the president to sell, exchange, or trade $50 billion in war materials to the Allied nations, principally Great Britain.

In addition to providing its allies with tanks, aircraft, and munitions, the Lend-Lease program also encompassed a whole range of raw materials, agricultural products, and foodstuffs, totaling about $50 billion. These children in England eat cheese sandwiches that came from the U.S.

Harry Hopkins was one of President Roosevelt's most trusted diplomatic advisers. In June 1941, he went to Moscow carrying a letter in which Roosevelt asked how the U.S. could most effectively "make available the assistance which the United States can render to your country in its magnificent resistance to the treacherous aggression by Hitlerite Germany...." FDR extended up to $1 billion lend-lease credit to the Soviet Union.

# Battle of Cape Matapan

Despite possessing some reasonably capable combat aircraft, such as this Macchi C.200 fighter, Italy's air force was in a perilous state. Even with twice as many airplanes as the British, it was easily overwhelmed during the desert campaign in Cyrenaica in 1940. Endemic inefficiency, excessive bureaucracy, and the exclusion of air force officers and experts from the aircraft selection and development process all contributed to the failure of Italian airpower.

A Royal Navy Fairey Fulmar flies air cover over the British fleet at the Battle of Cape Matapan off Crete on March 27–29, 1941. The combined force of British Royal Navy and Australian Navy ships protecting convoys bound for Greece engaged an Italian naval force. The heaviest fighting occurred on March 28. After the battle, the Italians temporarily conceded the eastern Mediterranean to the British, who could now concentrate more on the fighting in North Africa.

# Sinking of the *Hood* and Sinking of the *Bismarck*

The German battleship *Bismarck* fires toward the British battle cruiser *Hood* on May 24, 1941. According to Lieutenant Esmond Knight, who witnessed the attack, "a great spouting explosion issued from the centre of the *Hood*, enormous reaching tongues of pale-red flame shot into the air, while dense clouds of whitish-yellow smoke burst upwards, gigantic pieces of brightly burning debris being hurled hundreds of feet in the air.... *Hood* had literally been blown to pieces."

After sinking the *Hood* on May 24, 1941, and seriously damaging the *Prince of Wales*, the German battleship *Bismarck* (*pictured*) slipped away. British crews eagerly tried to catch the *Bismarck*, but with their ships running low on fuel, the British despaired of catching Germany's magnificent menace. On May 26, British torpedo planes slowed the ship down, but then lost it again. On the 27th, the *Bismarck* was finally sunk.

# Franklin Roosevelt Declares an Unlimited National Emergency

President Roosevelt considered Germany's naval threat to Atlantic shipping so serious that he declared an Unlimited National Emergency. Here, New York harbor workers transport mines to a mine-planter in July. This vessel belonged to the Army Mine Planter Service, part of the Coast Artillery Corps. Responsibility for East Coast defense fell to a growing number of authorities, including the Coast Guard, Inshore Patrol, Ship Lane Patrol, and Coastal Picket Patrol.

In 1940, Germany had a small but effective fleet of submarines, such as the U-boat *Krieg* seen here. German U-boats proved especially deadly against Allied merchant shipping. The fall of France provided a 2,500-mile coast from which to unleash U-boat "wolf packs" against still-unescorted transatlantic merchant convoys.

Oil barrels remain piled on the dock after President Franklin Roosevelt's declaration of an oil embargo on Japan in July 1941.

# U.S. Declares an Oil Embargo on Japan

apan's desire for economic independence and the establishment of a commanding presence in East Asia requires access to resources, particularly oil. On July 24, 1941, the quest to conquer these resources prompts Japanese forces to enter southern Indochina. President Roosevelt acts harshly, freezing Japanese assets and placing oil exports to Japan under restrictive licensing. This virtual embargo will be lifted only if the Japanese withdraw from China and Indochina and end their pact with the Axis powers. Under the American restriction, Japan will grow weaker as the Allies grow stronger.

In July 1941, Japanese forces occupied southern Indochina, where they met no opposition. When the American government tried to avert war in late 1941, one of its key demands was that the Japanese evacuate French Indochina.

# U-boat Torpedoes the USS *Kearny* in the North Atlantic

In July 1941, President Roosevelt sent troops to relieve British forces in Iceland. Soon after the Nazi occupation of Denmark in 1940, the British had moved into Iceland in order to keep northern sea lanes open. When British forces were needed elsewhere, U.S. troops took over the defense of the country.

The *Kearny* had gone to aid a slow convoy under wolf pack attack, but it became a target itself when it was silhouetted at night by the light of a torpedoed merchant ship and halted by passing traffic. The torpedo that hit its starboard side caused 11 deaths. A Navy Catalina (flying boat) dropped plasma to the ship by parachute. The *Kearny* returned to Iceland, escorted by the USS *Greer*. The latter's battle with *U-652* on September 4 had led to Roosevelt's "shoot on sight" policy against vessels interfering with American shipping.

# The U.S. Loses Its First Naval Vessel

During the war, combatants used radar to detect ships and planes far beyond the range of the human eye. It was the British who first used radar for a military advantage, as they built a series of radar stations along the English coast in 1938 to detect approaching aircraft.

The USS *Reuben James* was the first American naval vessel lost in World War II. It was one of five destroyers escorting a fast convoy when, about 600 miles west of Ireland on October 31, 1941, a torpedo from *U-552* struck it. The forepart of the ship was blown off as far back as the fourth of its characteristic four stacks. Only 45 of its crew of about 160 survived. Among the dead were all of the ship's officers, including the commanding officer, LCDR H. L. Edwards. This disaster prompted further amendments to the Neutrality Act.

# Japanese Planes Attack the U.S. Base at Pearl Harbor

t 8:00 A.M. on Sunday, December 7, 1941, nearly 200 Japanese carrier-borne aircraft attack Pearl Harbor in Hawaii. American casualties include 21 ships damaged or sunk and 3,600 men killed or wounded. One hundred and eighty-eight aircraft are destroyed, and 159 are damaged.

The Pearl Harbor attack leads to the merging of the aggressive wars of Japan and Germany and the involvement of the United States in a global war. The cry "Remember Pearl Harbor" resonates throughout the war.

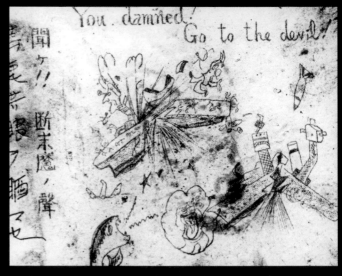

The men piloting the aircraft during the attack on Pearl Harbor had been trained in a culture in which loyalty unto death in the service of their emperor was a sacred principle. This cartoon depicts the zeal that they brought to their mission.

The U.S. battleships *West Virginia* and *Tennessee* (*both pictured*) were heavily damaged during the attack on Pearl Harbor.

U.S. Marines look skyward for Japanese planes at Ewa Marine Corps Air Station southwest of Pearl Harbor. Ewa came under air attack about two minutes before the main enemy raid struck Pearl Harbor.

DORIE MILLER
*Received the Navy Cross at Pearl Harbor, May 27, 1942*

Doris "Dorie" Miller was a mess attendant on the USS *West Virginia* the morning of the attack when he carried his mortally wounded captain to a safer spot on the ship. Although untrained, he proceeded to man a .50 caliber antiaircraft machine gun until ordered to abandon ship. He was awarded with the Navy Cross for his actions.

The USS *Arizona*, whose wreckage is pictured, was commissioned by the Navy in October 1916. Minutes after the attack began, the *Arizona* was hit by a 1,760-pound armor-piercing bomb. The explosive penetrated the deck and ignited more than a million pounds of gunpowder, tearing the ship apart and killing 1,177 members of the crew.

Many civilians, both men and women, worked for hours fighting fires on the ships and docks of Pearl Harbor.

# Franklin Roosevelt Signs a Declaration of War

n December 8, 1941, President Roosevelt makes an impassioned speech to Congress, calling for a declaration of war. His opening—"Yesterday, December 7, 1941, a date which will live in infamy…"—helps to stoke the American fever for revenge.

FDR signs the declaration in the Oval Office while surrounded by legislators and Cabinet members. Revisionist historians have claimed that Roosevelt had known about the attack and purposely withheld the information to provoke America's entry into the war. However, no evidence exists to support this assertion.

Hundreds of thousands of Americans enlisted in the armed forces in the weeks after the United States declared war on Japan. This number included sports figures and movie stars. "Rapid" Robert Feller, star pitcher of the Cleveland Indians, enlisted in the Navy two days after Pearl Harbor was attacked. The young men in this picture line up outside a Navy recruiting station in Boston on December 8, 1941. Many enlisted in the Navy in order to avoid the Army.

Crowds began to form in front of the White House as soon as word of the attack on Pearl Harbor was announced. The country sought reassurance from President Roosevelt that the country was safe in his hands.

# The Siege of Leningrad Begins

Hitler orders the obliteration of Leningrad and its people through bombing, shelling, starvation, and disease. He also forbids the acceptance of any surrender offer, if made. Field Marshal Leeb's Army Group North reaches Leningrad on September 8, 1941, and begins an 872-day German siege, during which close to a million of the city's citizens die.

As autumn 1941 drew to a close on the Eastern Front, soldiers began to suffer respiratory diseases, and sentries literally froze to death. Frostbite and cold-burn injuries escalated in –40°F temperatures.

A woman in Leningrad pulls the corpse of a child on a sleigh.

Although Leningrad was besieged by the Germans, Lake Ladoga to the northeast of Leningrad provided a lifeline for the starving population and military resources for the city's defenders. In summer, boats could traverse the lake, while in winter it froze hard, enabling supply trucks to drive across it (*pictured*).

# The U.S. and Britain Form the Combined Chiefs of Staff

Heading the British mission was Field Marshal Sir John Dill (*pictured, seventh from left*). Dill was instrumental in circumventing or defusing numerous issues and policy differences that could have disrupted Anglo-U.S. relations. Dill was lauded for his diplomacy, intellect, and achievements in Washington. When Dill died in post in 1944, he was accorded the unique honor of burial in the Arlington National Cemetery.

For the Allies to prosecute the war successfully, they need to establish and maintain a sound working relationship between the national military staffs of the U.S. and Great Britain at the strategic level. To achieve this, the U.S. Joint Chiefs of Staff and the British Chiefs of Staff form the Combined Chiefs of Staff in February 1942. The Combined Chiefs advise on, develop, modify, and direct Anglo-U.S. strategic policy on behalf of Churchill and Roosevelt.

# The British Surrender Singapore to the Japanese

In a scene that has come to symbolize the end of an empire, British officers prepare to surrender Singapore to the Japanese. The loss of the "Gibraltar of the Far East" on February 15, 1942, ranks among the greatest defeats in British military history. The quick Japanese victory over a numerically superior force stunned the world, shattered British military power in the region, exposed the myth of Western superiority for all to see, and raised the hopes of nationalist movements chafing under colonial rule.

Clouds of smoke roil into the sky following an air raid on Surabaya, Java, in the Dutch East Indies. The Japanese had long coveted the region's vast oil fields and refineries, and they moved to occupy Java soon after the fall of Singapore.

Women and children arrive in Britain after evacuating from Singapore. Confident of the impregnability of the fortress and fearful of creating panic, British authorities waited too long to begin the mass evacuation of civilians. As defeat loomed, all available ships were hastily loaded with fleeing civilians. As coordination broke down, the evacuation became a debacle. Enemy planes attacked the fleeing ships and thousands of civilians drowned. Others survived drowning only to be murdered by Japanese troops as they struggled ashore on Bangka Island.

Sister Vivian Bullwinkel, an Australian Army nurse, evacuated from Singapore before it fell. Her ship was sunk by Japanese aircraft off Bangka Island near Sumatra. After struggling ashore, Bullwinkel escaped into the jungle and eventually surrendered to Japanese sailors. She then endured three years of harsh imprisonment, attributing her survival to the friendship of fellow nurses and faith in Australia.

# The U.S. Begins Sending Japanese Americans to Internment Camps

n February 1942, President Roosevelt signs Executive Order 9066, paving the way for the forcible removal of Japanese Americans from the West Coast.

About 110,000 people of Japanese descent, more than 60 percent of whom are American citizens, are relocated to 10 inland War Relocation Camps. Limited to taking only what they can carry, the internees lose their homes, businesses, and personal possessions.

Japanese Americans were relocated into barracks such as these at Manzanar, California. Confinement to fenced camps that were overseen by armed guards and watchtowers was psychologically devastating to people who considered themselves good Americans.

An officer of the Royal Canadian Navy questions Japanese Canadian fisherman. When Canadians became afraid that fishermen of Japanese ancestry might be charting the Pacific coastline for the enemy, the government confiscated all Japanese fishing boats. In early 1942, Canada interned the nearly 23,000 Japanese Canadians who lived in British Columbia—about three quarters of whom were citizens—in 10 camps scattered throughout the nation.

Like the young people seen here, Japanese Americans were held under guard at assembly centers, where their baggage was inspected for forbidden items, such as cameras, shortwave radios, and guns. They were then bussed to camps east of the Sierra Nevada Mountains.

# Japanese Soldiers Lead the Bataan Death March

Hands tied behind their backs, these three Americans were among 78,000 American and Filipino troops who went into captivity on Bataan. Their starving and diseased conditions influenced Major General Edward King's decision to surrender, though he was unable to extract from the Japanese commanders a commitment to treat the prisoners compassionately. The Japanese decided to march the prisoners to Camp O'Donnell, some 65 miles away.

The trek from Bataan to Camp O'Donnell became known as the Bataan Death March. Japanese plans for the march did not take into account the exhaustion, starvation, and illness of the prisoners, who were thus sure to die in large numbers. Added to this neglect was active Japanese persecution. Some senior Japanese officers so despised the prisoners that they wanted them killed en masse. Field officers beheaded many with their swords, and Japanese common soldiers willfully buried prisoners alive or set fire to civilians who sought to aid those suffering.

Many thousands of POWs and untold numbers of civilians died at the hands of the Japanese armed forces during World War II. They were the victims of murder, disease, starvation, malnutrition, medical experiments, and overall neglect. The death rate for prisoners of war in Japanese hands ranged between 30 and 50 percent.

# Doolittle's Tokyo Raid

ed by Lieutenant Colonel James Doolittle, 16 B-25 bombers lumber off the deck of the American aircraft carrier *Hornet* and turn toward the Japanese coast, more than 600 miles away. Their top-secret mission: to carry out the first attack of the war on enemy homeland.

While the material damage inflicted is minimal, the Doolittle Raid lifts Allied morale and stuns the Japanese. No longer can the Japanese pretend that the homeland is inviolate.

B-25 bombers aboard the USS *Hornet*

A B-25 on its one-way bombing raid against Tokyo. The Army pilots had practiced short takeoffs from dry land, but none had ever tried it from a heaving carrier deck. An encounter with a Japanese picket boat forced the Doolittle Raiders to launch earlier than planned. Aided by a 50-mph headwind, all the B-25s got safely into the air, though many hung perilously close to the waves before gaining altitude.

Air crew members on the deck of the USS *Hornet* watch as Lieutenant Colonel James Doolittle wires a Japanese medal to a 500-pound bomb before the daring B-25 raid on Tokyo.

This aerial photo, snapped during the Doolittle Raid, reveals ships moored in Tokyo Bay. Most of the B-25s arrived over Tokyo just after noon on April 18. All the B-25s survived the actual raid, except for one that crash-landed in China after it ran out of fuel.

# The U.S. Government Creates the Office of War Information

he Office of War Information (OWI) is created to funnel information to the American media. The OWI concentrates on "selling" the war by manipulating pro-American sentiment and dehumanizing the enemy.

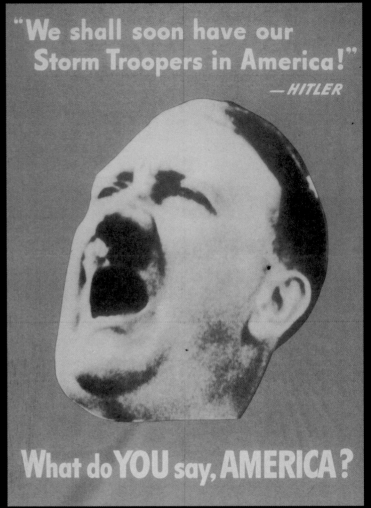

"We shall soon have our Storm Troopers in America!" —HITLER

What do YOU say, AMERICA?

Hitler was the subject of many propaganda posters, such as the one shown here. They often poked fun at his speeches, but underlying this humor lay a foundation of fear for those American who believed it possible for Germany and Japan to bring the war to North America.

The OWI sent story detectives to pulp magazines, as illustrated by this set-up photo with its heavy implications of sexual threat. In addition, rigid guidelines restricted what could appear in movies. With the OWI controlling what the American public read, saw, and heard, relevant information about the war was laced with propaganda.

On August 8, 1942, six German men, found guilty of espionage, were led individually to an electric chair in a District of Columbia jail. Two of the men revealed a plan to disrupt the manufacture of war materials to the FBI before any acts of sabotage could be carried out, and thus had their death penalties commuted by President Roosevelt. Richard Quirin (*pictured*) was one of the executed.

# The FBI's Role Expands

The Federal Bureau of Investigation (FBI) expands from 391 agents in 1933 to 3,000 agents in 1942.

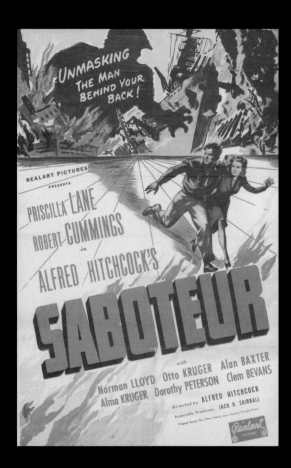

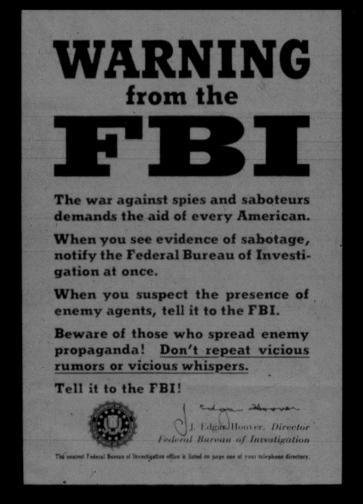

Not one instance of enemy sabotage occurred in the United States during the war–a testament, in part, to FBI vigilance. For the 1942 film, *Saboteur,* however, director Alfred Hitchcock supposed that such a crime did take place. In the film, an innocent shipyard worker becomes a fugitive.

When war broke out in Europe in 1939, the FBI's role was expanded to include sabotage and espionage investigations.

# The Allies Achieve Victory at the Battle of Midway

fter U.S. cryptologists break the Japanese naval code and discover the details of the enemy plan to seize U.S.-held Midway Island, the Americans set a trap. When the Japanese arrive on June 4 and begin their aerial attack on the island's defenders, the U.S. carriers *Yorktown*, *Enterprise*, and *Hornet* are waiting in ambush.

The Japanese suddenly find themselves under attack. Dive-bombers proceed to sink Japanese aircraft carriers *Akagi*, *Kaga*, *Soryo*, and *Hiryu*. Stunned by these losses, Admiral Yamamoto Isoroku orders withdrawal.

President Roosevelt chose Chester Nimitz (*pictured*) as commander-in-chief of the Pacific Fleet after Japan's attack on Pearl Harbor. Nimitz's first task was to rebuild the Pacific Fleet, a job he accomplished swiftly. Within six months of the attack, Nimitz achieved a stunning victory over the Japanese at the Battle of Midway.

Smoke billows from the USS *Yorktown* following Japanese air attacks at Midway. The carrier survived three bomb hits and two torpedoes before the crew was ordered to abandon ship. Hours later, a Japanese submarine sent two more torpedoes into the carrier. *Yorktown* sank the following morning.

Many historians consider the Battle of Midway the most significant naval engagement of World War II. The battle turned back a Japanese attempt to seize Midway Atoll and destroy the U.S. fleet in a decisive confrontation. The Imperial Japanese Navy would never regain the superiority it had enjoyed over the first six months of the war.

A U.S. Navy Douglas SBD Dauntless dive-bomber releases part of its payload. Dauntless was credited with sinking more Japanese warships than any other U.S. aircraft type from 1941 to 1943. At Midway alone, Dauntless dive-bombers sank four Japanese carriers and damaged two heavy cruisers

# U.S. Invades Guadalcanal

After U.S. Intelligence discovers a Japanese airfield under construction on Guadalcanal, the First Marine Division interrupts its training in Australia and hastily ships out to seize the island.

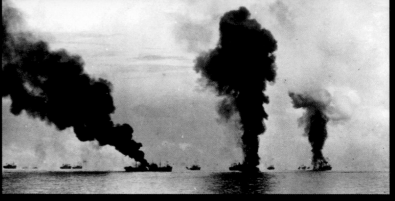

Crashed aircraft and the transport USS *George F. Elliott* burn off Guadalcanal on August 8, 1942, following an attack by Japanese bombers and torpedo planes.

American Marines storm ashore from a landing craft at Guadalcanal. The landing by more than 11,000 Marines took the 2,571 Japanese–mostly laborers working on the airfield–by surprise. Most of the enemy fled into the jungle as the Marines stormed ashore.

The USS *North Carolina*, the first of the U.S. Navy's modern battleships, participated in the invasion of Guadalcanal. Its role was to screen carriers from air and surface attack and use its guns to soften enemy island defenses prior to amphibious assault. The *North Carolina* received 15 battle stars for service during the war.

A crashed Japanese bomber floats off Tulagi. U.S. Marines invaded the small island, located just 20 miles north of Guadalcanal, on August 7, 1942, to secure its valuable harbor. By August 8, the Marines had pushed the defenders into the southeastern part of the island, where they were annihilated.

# Japanese Torpedoes Sink the USS *Wasp*

It was common for the OWI to use a stereotypical image of Japanese soldiers with slanted eyes engaged in evil acts. Here we see a frightening depiction of a Japanese soldier with very sharp features carrying, apparently, an American woman from a scene portraying hell. The message was that unless the Allies stopped the Japanese in the Pacific, horrors like this would happen in America.

Mortally wounded, the carrier USS *Wasp* burns after taking three torpedo hits from the Japanese submarine *I-19*. Commissioned in 1940, the *Wasp* was a smaller model of the larger *Yorktown* class carriers. Prior to the war, it engaged in Atlantic patrol duty and ferried RAF planes sent to Malta. Sent to the Pacific in June 1942, the *Wasp* participated in the Guadalcanal landings and later provided cover for resupply convoys to the Solomons. It was sunk by the *I-19* southeast of San Cristobol Island while escorting troop transports to Guadalcanal.

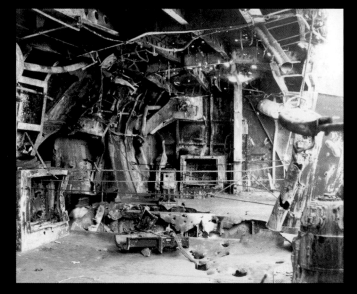

# Battle of the Santa Cruz Islands

The Santa Cruz engagement pits two U.S. carriers and support ships against four Japanese carriers and their support. U.S. pilots damage two enemy carriers and a cruiser, but the carrier USS *Hornet* and a destroyer are sunk in the exchange. The Japanese claim a tactical victory, but their failure to crush U.S. naval forces in the Solomons leaves the strategic advantage with the Americans. Indeed, Japanese losses in precious first-line aircrews make the battle a far greater defeat than Midway.

The USS *Enterprise* survived bomb strikes in Midway, the Doolittle Raid, and the Battle of Santa Cruz, as well as several more battles. The *Enterprise* survived the war and was decommissioned in 1947.

A Japanese torpedo plane approaches the battleship USS *South Dakota* during the Battle of the Santa Cruz Island.

# Allied Forces Launch Operation Torch

The 1942 Operation Torch landings in French North Africa involve more than 500 vessels and 65,000 men. The landing craft include early-model Higgins boats, some without ramps. However, British craft predominate.

British admiral Sir Andrew Browne Cunningham commanded the Naval Task Forces during Operation Torch under General Dwight Eisenhower, who praised Cunningham for his intelligence, devotion, and selflessness.

Allied forces make an amphibious landing near Algiers. Few American troops based in Europe had been under fire, and they did not know whether Vichy French defenders would resist the landings. Military considerations aside, Torch was tricky politically because Stalin was insisting that U.S. and British forces commit significant numbers of men to European combat with an invasion of France. Roosevelt and Churchill knew such an assault was not yet possible, and offered Torch as a substitute.

Roosevelt supported the British plan to invade North Africa in order to engage the Germans as soon as possible. French Morocco and Algeria were chosen as the sites for the attack since the Allies would face only French troops, who might let the Allies land unopposed. That is not how it turned out. After the November 8, 1942, landing, the French troops did defend the landing sites. Here, a British ship takes a hit not far from shore.

# Germans Invade Stalingrad

The German attempt to seize Stalingrad in the summer of 1942 turns into one of the epic battles of World War II and one of the bloodiest battles in history. The battle for the city rages for five months, during which the advance of the Axis powers is halted and crushed. By the time General Friedrich Paulus surrenders in early February 1943, the tide has begun to turn not just on the Eastern Front, but also in the Middle East and the Pacific.

When German troops reached the suburbs of Stalingrad on August 23, 1942, they found little more than ruins. But German claims to victory were cut short by Russian soldiers and civilians fighting back from those remains. The war broke down into smaller battles in which, as a German general said, "The mile, as a measure of distance, was replaced by the yard. . . ." Here, in the fall of 1942, Soviet soldiers fight the enemy in an area already devastated by warfare.

Ferocious Soviet resistance at Stalingrad stalled the German military juggernaut that had smashed through Russia. Even though German bombardment had turned 80 percent of the city to burnt rubble and killed tens of thousands of civilians, the Soviets held fast—as depicted here by cartoonist Leslie Illingworth.

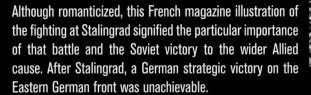

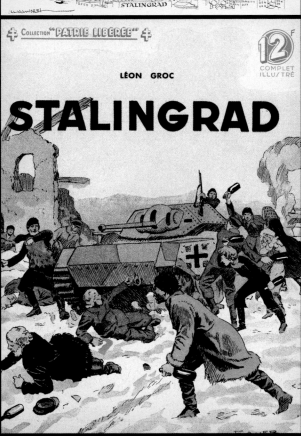

Although romanticized, this French magazine illustration of the fighting at Stalingrad signified the particular importance of that battle and the Soviet victory to the wider Allied cause. After Stalingrad, a German strategic victory on the Eastern German front was unachievable.

German troops surrender at Stalingrad.

# Hitler's Death Camps

The first Nazi death camps are started in 1933 and dedicated to the systematic extermination of their inmates in accordance with the plan for a "Final Solution" of the "Jewish question."

Auschwitz is the most notorious of the Nazi death camps in Poland, whose overall purpose is the extermination of Europe's Jews, together with the Sinti and Roma people, homosexuals, and many other groups considered socially, politically, or racially undesirable. Treblinka, Sobibór, Majdanek, Belzec, and Chelmno are the other main extermination camps. These extermination camps are designed to kill on an industrialized scale, this being achieved most efficiently through the use of gas chambers. The resulting corpses are burned in purpose-built crematoriums.

About four million people die in the extermination camps.

Jews at Auschwitz

At Ravensbrük, a camp primarily for women from many different nationalities, religions, and lifestyles, medical experiments were conducted on helpless inmates. This picture of Polish inmate Bogumila Babinska, smuggled out of the camp, shows the effect of four deep cuts on her thigh muscles.

Jews huddle together at Auschwitz. This German complex in southern Poland included three concentration camps and 36 subcamps. Auschwitz I contained Polish political prisoners, Auschwitz II (Birkenau) was the extermination camp, and Auschwitz III was a forced-labor camp. Birkenau contained gas chambers and a crematorium that could dispose of 2,000 bodies at a time.

Before Jews and other enemies of the Third Reich were exterminated at the Treblinka death camp in Poland, their shoes (and other possessions) were confiscated. More than 700,000 Jews died at Treblinka, a death toll exceeded only at Auschwitz.

# Allies Prevail in North Africa

n May 6, 1943, the Allies launch their last offensive against the Axis in North Africa. On May 13, the German and Italian troops in Tunisia surrender. This is the first major success of the alliance between America and Britain.

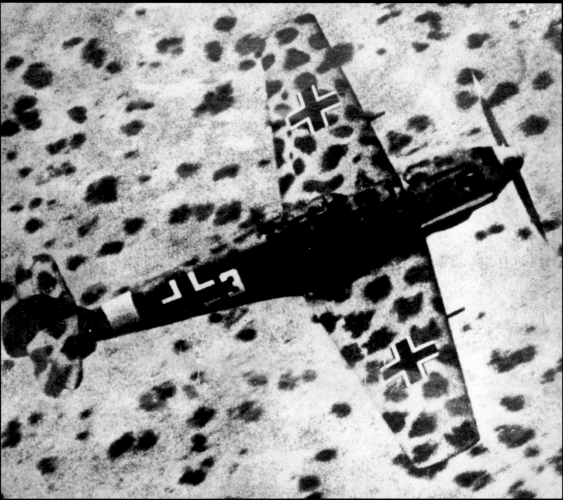

THE GOVERNMENTS OF THE UNITED STATES AND GREAT BRITAIN Present

## TUNISIAN VICTORY

THE INVASION AND LIBERATION OF NORTH AFRICA

AN OFFICIAL RECORD PRODUCED BY BRITISH AND AMERICAN SERVICE FILM UNITS
DISTRIBUTED BY THE BRITISH MINISTRY OF INFORMATION        Metro Goldwyn Mayer RELEASE

A German Messerschmitt Me-109 is camouflaged to blend in with the African desert. Prior to February 1941, the fight for North Africa was waged between British and Italian forces. The arrival of German divisions commanded by General Erwin Rommel tipped the scales in Italy's favor. The equalizer for British troops was the superiority of its air force over the German *Luftwaffe*. The greatest threat to both Allied and Axis aircraft was the damage inflicted by sand and the torrid climate.

To promote the success of the Allies, director Frank Capra prepared this 75-minutes documentary of the North Africa campaign, beginning with Operation Torch and ending with the fall of Tunisia.

# The British Royal Air Force Launches Operation Chastise

With a new type of bomb, the RAF attacks three dams that supply water to the German industries of the Ruhr. The dam raids boost British morale more than they damage the German war effort. Perhaps the most significant result is the creation of the elite 617 Squadron demonstrating the value of giving highly trained aircrew specialized weapons.

Guy Gibson (*fourth from left*) led the 19 planes of Operation Chastise on their mission to blow up dams. For his leadership and valor, Gibson was awarded the Victoria Cross, the highest British military award.

Invented by aeronautical engineer Barnes Wallis, the cylindrical "bouncing bomb" needed to "skip" across the lake surface to slide down the dam wall and explode. This photograph shows the Eder dam after it was bombed.

# The British and the U.S. Launch the Combined Bomber Offensive

The Combined Bomber offensive is officially launched as Operation Pointblank in June 1943. The offensive is aimed at the enemy's military-economic complex—the source of German airpower and the morale of the urban workforce.

Over the course of the war, more than 420,000 German civilians die from the bombing attacks. A further 60,000 civilians are killed in attacks on Italian cities. The bomb attacks immediately affect German strategy. To establish a defense sector, the Germans have to withdraw valuable resources of manpower, artillery, shells, and aircraft from the military front line.

Pictured are civilians killed in a bombing raid on Hamburg, Germany.

On July 27–29, 1942, the Allies dropped high-explosive and incendiary bombs on Hamburg, Germany. The attacks killed more than 45,000 civilians and soldiers and left more than a million residents homeless.

On February 15, 1944, Allied bombers destroyed the historical abbey of Monte Cassino in Cassino, Italy. After the bombing, German troops moved into the ruins and defended them. During the brutal months that followed, the Allies demolished Cassino, finally capturing the city in May. Here, victorious British and South African soldiers and engineers pose amid Cassino's ruins with a captured Nazi flag.

The German port city of Wilhelmshaven was bombed twice in 1943. These aerial reconnaissance images show Wilhelmshaven before and after the two bombings.

# The Soviets Claim Victory at the Battle of Kursk

n May and June of 1943, a vast army of Soviet civilians turns the Kursk salient into a veritable fortress. The Red Army numbers 1.3 million, the Germans 900,000. On July 5, German forces begin the attack. They make slow progress over the first week against determined Soviet resistance. For the first time in the two years of fighting on the Eastern Front, a large-scale German campaign is held and then reversed without the crisis and retreat that have preceded other victories.

During the battle, nearly 1,000 artillery pieces pummeled the German position. The barrage was answered by German guns and then the approach of German tanks. As the Germans advanced, however, they were met with very stiff resistance. In this picture, a distraught German soldier sits with his battered artillery piece and a dead comrade.

Soviet soldiers and tanks advance during the battle.

A Russian T-34 tank rolls through a burning village during the Battle of Kursk in July 1943. Anticipating the German offensive, the Soviets absorbed the blow with a network of well-prepared defensive lines, then counterattacked. The counterblow drove the German army out of central and southern Russia and opened the way to victory in the East.

# Allies Invade Sicily

fter the Axis defeat in North Africa, the Allies' next objective becomes the enemy's airfields and ports in Sicily. They also hope that the fall of Sicily will force Italy out of the war. The plan calls for American and Allied paratroopers to jump on the evening of July 9–10, followed the next morning by one of the largest amphibious landings of the war with 160,000 British troops, 600 tanks, and 1,800 artillery pieces.

Sicily was defended by some 300,000 Italian and 40,000 German troops with 50 tanks and 200 pieces of artillery. Here, an Italian soldier mans a gun post on the coast.

Rough terrain and the stubborn resistance of German troops slowed the Allied advance across Sicily. Oppressive heat (100°F) also affected the advance. More than 10,000 Allied soldiers became sick with heat exhaustion and malaria.

General George Patton was determined to show the British the fighting skills of his men at Sicily. "This is a horse race in which the prestige of the U.S. Army is at stake," he wrote to General Troy Middleton, his 45th Division commander. On July 22, Patton's men took Palermo, as seen in this picture, making it the first West European city to by liberated. Allied troops were greeted like this throughout Sicily.

# The Manhattan Project

t the outbreak of war, Germany is the only nation with a military office dedicated to future applications of nuclear energy. However, American physicists recognize that fission's accompanying energy release has military potential. Roosevelt establishes a committee of scientists to determine the feasibility of an American nuclear weapon. The project becomes known as the Manhattan Project.

The presence of brilliant American physicist J. Robert Oppenheimer attracted scientists from all over the world to a remote New Mexican desert to work on the Manhattan Project. Oppenheimer directed the scientific team headquartered at Los Alamos. He, like most Los Alamos scientists, was dedicated to ending war for all time.

Manhattan Project workers at a test site in Los Alamos

In 1943, hundreds of families moved to the highly secret Los Alamos National Laboratory community in New Mexico, where the first atomic bomb was built. Workers lived in simple housing (*pictured*), although those higher in the scientific hierarchy had proportionately better homes. Los Alamos residents worked hard and relaxed at movies, restaurants, and parties within the compound.

U.S. brigadier general Leslie Groves named the Manhattan Project and was a driving force behind the creation of the first atomic bomb.

# Mussolini Loses Power and Italy Surrenders

n July 25, 1943, having lost the support of fellow politicians, his own military, and a majority of the Fascist Grand Council, Mussolini is ousted in a bloodless coup. On September 3, 1943, Italy signs a treaty with American officials in Sicily, effectively surrendering to the Allies. Once Hitler learns of Italy's surrender, he orders the German occupation of his onetime ally and the arrest of all Italian troops.

After Italy's government surrendered, a sprawling Italian resistance movement sprang up against German occupation. It consisted of a loose network of Catholics, Jews, Communists, and other groups. These Italians, pictured in Sicily, aided South African troops in locating German snipers.

As he reshaped Germany's government and society in the 1930s, Hitler turned to Benito Mussolini as a mentor for implementing his Fascist reforms. The situation changed when Mussolini was deposed and imprisoned in July 1943. Hitler arranged for Mussolini's rescue and installed him as head of a puppet Fascist government. However, he no longer considered Mussolini a mentor or an equal.

When Italy surrendered, there was much celebration in America's Italian communities (such as this one in New York), for many had immigrated to escape Mussolini and his Fascist policies.

# American Forces Land on Bougainville

U.S. troops clamber into assault boats assembling for the landing on Bougainville, the largest of the Solomon Islands. Part of the effort to neutralize the Japanese base at Rabaul 220 miles away, the landing was spearheaded at Cape Torokina. Though the Japanese had some 17,000 troops on southern Bougainville alone, they had not considered swampy Cape Torokina a likely target, and the landing was lightly opposed.

American troops operate amid dead bodies on Bougainville. Roadblocks, ambushes, and terrifying patrol encounters at point-blank range in the thick jungle were routine. Japanese machine gunners sheltered in well-concealed log and earthen bunkers had to be reduced one by one by infantrymen using hand grenades, small arms, and flamethrowers.

General Alexander Archer Vandegrift, nicknamed "Sunny Jim" for his upbeat personality and courteous style, gained acclaim as the commander of the First Marine Division at Guadalcanal. He later commanded the First Marine Amphibious Corps in the landings at Bougainville.

American soldiers advance with a Sherman tank during the fighting on Bougainville.

# Roosevelt, Churchill, and Stalin Hold the Tehran Conference

he Big Three—Roosevelt, Churchill, and Stalin—meet only twice during the war. The first time is in Tehran, Iran. For more than a year, Stalin has demanded the invasion of France to force Germany to shift resources to the West. In Tehran, Roosevelt and Churchill announce their decision to invade France in May 1944. Stalin agrees to simultaneously mount an aggressive offense in the East. He also pressures his allies to accept some of his demands, including Soviet possession of the eastern part of postwar Poland and his veto on the plan to divide postwar Germany into five autonomous states. It is also determined at the conference that the Soviets will join the fight against Japan after Germany is defeated.

Ideologically, Churchill and Stalin were diametrically opposed to each other. However, war had made them comrades in adversity. Despite their philosophical differences, they developed a unique personal relationship that subsequently ensured the Allied victory.

Stalin, Roosevelt, and Churchill meet in Tehran, Iran.

# The Bombing of Berlin

In a November 1943 letter to Winston Churchill concerning a planned bombing of Berlin, British air marshal Sir Arthur Harris states, "It will cost Germany the war." The bombing of Germany's largest city begins on November 18 and lasts until the end of March 1944. Although the attacks kill more than 10,000 civilians and leave hundreds of thousands homeless, they fail to destroy the city or the morale of its citizens.

Britain's Avro Lancaster bombers participated in every major night raid on Germany, and carried bigger loads and heavier bombs than any other aircraft in Europe. Approximately 7,300 of these bombers were constructed by war's end.

Bodies of citizens wait to be identified in a Berlin gymnasium decorated for Christmas.

# The Battle for Tarawa

The Second Marine Division has fought in the Solomons, but the amphibious assault on tiny, heavily defended Tarawa is a new experience. Japanese rear admiral Shibasaki Keiji boasts that "a million Americans couldn't take Tarawa in a hundred years." Defenses include barbed wire, mines, tetrahedrons, pillboxes, tanks, machine guns, and naval rifles. Thanks to the stubborn courage of individual Marines, Shibasaki is proven wrong, but the cost is high. More than 1,000 Americans are killed or go missing.

Dead Marines litter the beach following the 76-hour battle for Betio (at the southwest corner of Tarawa Atoll) and its strategically important airstrip. The Tarawa assault was a costly learning experience. Marines were shot down by the hundreds as they waded toward the heavily defended landing beaches. "It was a time of utmost savagery," wrote a witness. "I still don't know how they took the place."

Draped with hand grenades and ammunition, a Marine pauses to drink from his canteen during the fight for Tarawa.

—*TIME-LIFE* CORRESPONDENT ROBERT SHERROD, DESCRIBING A MOMENT
DURING THE BATTLE FOR TARAWA, NOVEMBER 20, 1943

Trapped in their bunker in Tarawa, these two Japanese Special Naval Landing Force troops chose suicide over surrender.

# The Allies Liberate Rome

he Allies march on Rome, one day after Hitler orders his armies withdrawn. Though sporadic fighting occurs in the outskirts, the city center is spared.

In 1943, *Time* magazine praised Pope Pius XII and the Catholic Church for "fighting totalitarianism more knowingly, devoutly, and authoritatively, and for a longer time, than any other organized power." However, even during his life, Pius's wartime policies were controversial. Despite his muted denunciations of Nazi aggression and racial theories, the Vatican under his leadership remained officially neutral throughout the war. Pius also stirred criticism for not denouncing the Nazis' atrocities against the Jews. Members of the Church hierarchy, however, hid Jews in monasteries, convents, and the Vatican itself, saving thousands of Jewish lives.

Shortly before the liberation of Rome (*pictured*), the city had endured a week of Allied bombings that killed some 5,000 civilians. Even so, crowds of Romans grateful for an end to the Nazi occupation joyfully greeted the soldiers of U.S. general Mark Clark's Fifth Army, showering them with flowers. On June 5, President Roosevelt reminded Americans that Ancient Rome had once ruled the known world. "That, too, is significant," he said, "for the United Nations are determined that in the future no one city and no on race will be able to control the whole of the world."

# D-Day

n an awesome show of military force, the Allies land on the coast of France in an amphibious invasion known as D-Day. German positions in Normandy are bombarded with more than 175,000 troops, 600 warships, and nearly 10,000 bombers and other warplanes. By the end of the month, nearly a million Allies are on French soil.

Most Americans were anxious for news of D-Day, as seen in this scene from New York City. President Roosevelt emphasized in a news conference that the invasion did not mean the fighting was almost over. "You don't just walk to Berlin," he said, "and the sooner this country realizes that, the better."

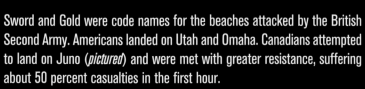

Sword and Gold were code names for the beaches attacked by the British Second Army. Americans landed on Utah and Omaha. Canadians attempted to land on Juno (*pictured*) and were met with greater resistance, suffering about 50 percent casualties in the first hour.

Americans advance over a sea wall after landing on Utah beach. Allies met with the stiffest resistance on Juno and Omaha beaches. U.S. colonel George Taylor of the First Infantry Division tried to motivate his shell-shocked men to advance off Omaha. "Two kinds of people are staying on this beach," he said, "the dead and those who are going to die."

A Normandy beach two days after D-Day

# U.S. Marines Land on the Mariana Islands

nvading the Mariana Islands, from which U.S. bombers can bomb Japan, is an immense challenge. Some 535 combat ships and auxiliaries transport 127,571 troops to islands more than a thousand miles from the nearest base, Eniwetok. The Marianas are 3,500 miles from the troops' departure point, Pearl Harbor. On June 15, 1944, more than 600 amphibious craft debark two divisions on eight beaches on a four-mile front with no serious collisions. Some 8,000 Marines are landed in the first 20 minutes. Once the troops are ashore, they meet fierce resistance.

A Marine works a field telephone switchboard at a temporary command post on Mount Tapochau in the center of Saipan. The capture of Tapochau by the Second Marine Division on June 25 was a turning point. Efficient American communications on Saipan contributed enormously to the complex invasion's eventual success.

Vessels such as this landing craft carried Marines to the key Mariana island, Saipan.

Saipan's terrain was much more diverse than the small, low-lying atolls of the Marine's and Army's recent campaigns. Mountains, tangled vegetation, cane fields, ravines, and caves all presented obstacles. The enemy usually proved difficult to locate, and fighting everywhere was at close quarters.

During the initial landings on Saipan, Marines listened as chaplains gave them a prayer and blessing over the ships' loudspeakers. Here, an American pauses before a crucifix in a small cemetery.

The corpse of one of the 23,811 Japanese known to have died on Saipan leans back on a tree as if asleep.

# Allies Discover Death Camps

s the Allies advance on Germany from the east and west, they reach the Nazis' concentration camps and death camps. The Soviets become the first of the Allies to discover one of these scenes of horror when they enter the Majdanek concentration/death camp near Lublin, Poland.

Here, Russian soldiers and Polish civilians appear to be overcome by the sights and smells of death. Approximately 360,000 prisoners, mostly Jews, died at Majdanek from gas, hanging, starvation, disease, or overwork. The Red Army discovered only 500 inmates still alive at the camp.

German security forces lead Polish women to their execution in the Palmiry Forest. The Nazis spread their plans for genocide throughout each occupied country, killing Jews, political opponents, and anyone else they believed was a threat or an inferior to the Aryan race. German officers showed pictures like this to their troops in order to dehumanize the victims, making it easier for the troops to perform their gruesome assignments.

# The Liberation of Paris

n August 25, 1944, refusing to destroy the city as Hitler has ordered, German general Dietrich von Choltitz surrenders Paris to General Jacques-Philippe Leclerc and the Free French forces. French Communist Resistance fighters seek to take power, but Gaullist groups jockey into that position.

French general Charles de Gaulle makes a triumphant return to Paris on August 26, 1944. Ignoring sniper fire that sometimes scattered his admirers, the man who had led the Free French from exile in London walked down the *Champs Elysées* and visited the *Cathédrale Notre Dame de Paris*. De Gaulle moved back into his old office at the War Ministry and proclaimed the continuation of the Third Republic. He thus derailed an establishment of an Allied military government in France.

Armed resistance fighters maintain their guard during the liberation of Paris. The French Resistance included groups of students, Communists, liberals, anarchists, and Roman Catholics. When the Allies approached Paris, Resistance cells organized strikes by police and other city workers. They fought skirmishes with German forces even after Choltitz surrendered. About 1,500 Resistance members and other civilians were killed during the fight for liberation.

Parisians cheer as Allied tanks roll past the *Arc de Triomphe*. French citizens hoped that Americans were bringing food, clothes, and gasoline, which had been in short supply during Nazi rule, but such items were also in short supply among the liberators.

# The Allies Invade Germany

As Russia's Red Army raced into Germany from the east, officer leadership and troop discipline frequently broke down. In October 1944, units of Russia's 11th Guards Army rampaged through the East Prussian village of Nemmersdorf, nailing men to barns, raping women, and crushing the heads of infants. Russian atrocities of this sort prompted countless German civilians to make dangerous treks westward, in hopes of capture by relatively even-tempered American forces.

Two German prisoners of war, guarded by an American soldier, wait to be taken to a POW camp after the U.S. victory at Aachen, the first German city to fall to the Allies. For seven days, fighting had raged, with enemy snipers on rooftops picking off scores of U.S. soldiers. While American tanks struggled through debris-strewn streets to dislodge defenders, German soldiers and civilians took to cellars and sewers. The strategically unimportant city cost each side some 5,000 casualties, and about 5,600 Germans were taken prisoner.

General Dwight Eisenhower's three army groups reached the German border in September 1944 with superior forces and firepower. However, they were slowed by acute gasoline and ammunition shortages, as well as by determined German troops. To make matters worse, the American advance came during the wet season; daily cold rain turned the rough terrain to mud. By early October, when U.S. soldiers (*pictured*) drove into Germany, front-line American commanders realized that the German homeland would not be occupied quickly.

# U.S. Prevails at Leyte

fter two months of fighting, from October to December, U.S. forces secure the Philippine island of Leyte as part of General MacArthur's promise to win back the Philippines. American casualties are higher than anticipated, but the Japanese fare worse. The naval engagements off Leyte effectively destroy the remnants of the Japanese Navy, while the ground campaign consumes nearly 65,000 troops. In a last-grasp effort, Japanese paratroopers jump on two U.S. airfields on Leyte on December 6. Despite creating considerable confusion, all are killed or driven off.

American troops regard the bodies of Japanese snipers on the island of Leyte.

Early in the Pacific war, the Allies noted a Japanese willingness to die in battle. When Japan's strategic situation became dire, its leaders methodically exploited that enthusiasm. Vice Admiral Onishi Takijiro instigated aerial suicide attacks on enemy ships at Leyte Gulf in October 1944. The suicide units were called "*kamikaze*." *Kamikaze* attacks appealed to the Japanese command because they negated pilot inexperience and aircraft obsolescence, and reduced fuel consumption. There was no shortage of volunteers, such as the young pilot pictured here.

American submarines were a key factor in Japan's defeat. They sank nearly two-thirds of all the Japanese merchant tonnage that was destroyed and nearly one-third of all combatant ships that were sunk. Pictured is the USS *Wahoo*, a 1,525-ton *Gato*-class submarine.

Fire burns out of control on the aircraft carrier USS *Princeton* after a Japanese air attack. More than 60 land-based Japanese bombers and torpedo planes, escorted by 130 fighters, attacked U.S. naval forces covering the Leyte landings on October 24.

# The Battle of the Bulge

n December 16, 1944, Germany begins a massive attack in the Ardennes region of southern Belgium. The Germans force a "bulge" in the faltering Allied advance, plunging surprised U.S. forces into some of the fiercest fighting they will endure in Europe. U.S. forces do not call the engagement the Battle of the Bulge in its early days, instead referring to it as the German Breakthrough.

A German commando, captured wearing an American uniform during the Battle of the Bulge, prepares to face a firing squad. Small groups of these commandos, riding captured American jeeps and wearing GI uniforms, managed to penetrate U.S. lines in the early hours of the attack. Considered spies, those unfortunate enough to be captured were shot.

Weather was the Allies' worst handicap during the first days of the Battle of the Bulge—and the Germans knew it. They deliberately began their attack when poor visibility restricted air support for U.S. ground forces. Most of the battle's staggering number of American casualties took place during the first three days.

German soldiers advance past a knocked-out U.S. halftrack during the Battle of the Bulge. Intended to divide the Western Allies, Hitler's ill-advised counteroffensive was halted and then thrown back with great losses of men and irreplaceable equipment. After the Bulge, Germany's defeat was clearly just a matter of months.

U.S. soldiers watch Allied and German planes battle on Christmas Day, 1944. The weather over Belgium had cleared, and Allied aircraft were finally able to support ground troops in a counterattack against the Germans. The Battle of the Bulge had been frightfully costly to all combatants. American casualties numbered about 81,000, and German casualties were between 60,000 and 100,000. But Germany's loss of men and materiel was irreparable.

# The Malmedy Massacre

On Sunday, December 17, 1944, a number of American prisoners are shot by soldiers of the First SS-Panzer Regiment at Baugnez crossroads, close to the Belgian town of Malmedy. Of the 113 prisoners assembled in the field at Baugnez, 67 die there. Forty-six of them, some of whom are wounded, manage to escape the scene.

The massacre begins when some of the Germans open fire. A storm of machine gun and rifle fire lasts for 15 minutes, and is followed by deliberate shots to finish off anyone still showing signs of life. These final murderous *coups de grâce* turn a possible "battle incident" into an indisputable atrocity that resonates throughout the American forces in Northwest Europe. The massacre immediately prompts orders in some U.S. Army units to summarily shoot any SS prisoners they might capture.

Although those believed responsible for the massacre are later tried by a U.S. military tribunal, serious coercive and procedural irregularities by the prosecution eventually result in the commutation of all of the many death sentences.

"A bullet went through the head of the man next to me. I lay tensely still, expecting the end. Could he see me breathing? Could I take a kick in the groin without wincing?... He was standing at my head. What was he doing? Time seemed to stand still. And then I heard him reloading his pistol in a deliberate manner...laughing and talking. A few odd steps before the reloading was finished, and he was no longer so close to my head. I heard another shot a little farther away, and he had passed me up."

–U.S. ARMY FIRST LIEUTENANT VIRGIL T. LARY, DESCRIBING THE INCIDENT AT MALMEDY

The bodies of 67 American POWs lie in the Belgian snow. Those who escaped the Malmedy massacre reported the cold-blooded killings, and word reached U.S. front-line troops quickly. Apparently in response, a December 21 written order from the U.S. 328th Infantry Regiment read: "No SS troops or paratroopers will be taken prisoner but will be shot on sight."

GIs discovering the massacred POWs

# The Allies Bomb Nuremberg

uremberg is an important manufacturing center for the German war effort. It becomes a target for Allied bombing raids, and on January 2, 1945, the center of the city is attacked by Allied bombers.

The raid was so successful that most of the town's center was destroyed in less than an hour. More than 1,800 residents of Nuremberg were killed and thousands were left homeless.

Though shaken and angered by Allied bomb attacks on German cities, Hitler rarely visited targeted areas. Nevertheless, London's *News Chronicle* ran this photograph in its January 31, 1945, edition, with a caption claiming that the *Führer* "is surveying ruins of a German town, the name of which is not disclosed." The paper overlooked the fact that Hitler stopped wearing the swastika armband as soon as the war began. The photo is almost certainly from a visit to a prewar natural disaster or accident.

Liberation came too late for this sick and malnourished American POW at the Davao Penal Colony on Mindanao in the Philippines. He died while trying to get a drink of water from a sink in the camp hospital. Of the approximately 25,000 U.S. troops captured during the war, more than 10,000 died while in Japanese hands.

Reduced to skin and bones by three years of captivity, American civilians Lee Rogers (*left*) and John C. Todd sit outside the gym at Santo Tomas University in Manila. Santo Tomas was the primary internment center for American civilians following the fall of the Philippines, housing an average of about 4,000 internees. Though the civilians at Santo Tomas and other camps suffered from food shortages and overcrowding, they endured less brutality than Allied military prisoners and even managed to set up a school for the children.

# The Red Army Liberates Auschwitz

As the Red Army pushed westward in Poland, it arrived at the Auschwitz camp complex on January 27, 1945. "I saw the faces of the people we liberated," Soviet major Anatoly Shapiro recalled. "They went through hell." Nine days before the liberation, 60,000 prisoners had been marched from the Auschwitz complex to the other camps out of the immediate reach of Soviet troops. About 7,000 inmates were left behind and freed.

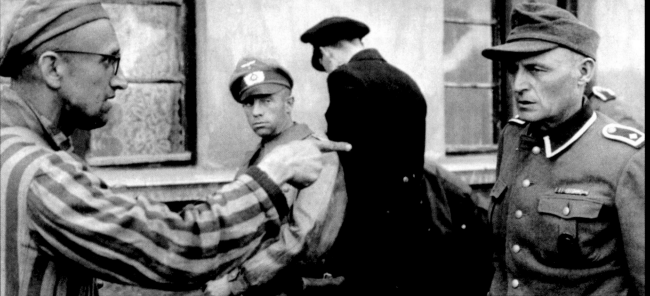

Allied troops advanced so quickly across Germany that many SS guards in slave and concentration camps were unable to escape. Others chose to face the enemy. Those guards who remained behind were immediately arrested once the Allies arrived. Liberated prisoners were taken to neighboring towns in an attempt to identify SS troopers who had abandoned their uniforms in attempt to mingle with civilians.

# The Yalta Conference

Roosevelt, Churchill, and Stalin met for the second and last time at Yalta on the Crimean Peninsula. In negotiations for the fate of Germany and Eastern Europe, Stalin had the advantage since most of that area was already in Soviet hands. He was, therefore, able to violate the promises he made about free elections in Poland and democratic governments in the liberated states of Central and Southeastern Europe. The Soviet leader confirmed his prior promise to enter the war against Japan. Stalin also reduced his demand for all 16 Soviet republics to be represented in the United Nations to two: the Ukraine and Belorussia.

# The Allies Firebomb Dresden

he beautiful German city of Dresden is known as the "Florence of the Elbe" before it suffers a series of bombings in 1945. The heaviest of these is conducted by British and American aircraft from February 13 to 15. The bombings cause firestorms that destroy much of the city and kill approximately 30,000 people.

Arthur Travers Harris, the head of the Royal Air Force Bomber Command, implemented area bombing—the indiscriminate destruction of cities instead of specific military targets. Harris believed that this tactic would destroy enemy morale and force Germany to surrender. The bombing of Dresden was his most controversial action.

During the war, approximately 50 percent of Germany's infrastructure was destroyed. Dresden was one of the hardest hit cities. Following the war, the ruins were cleared and replaced by modern structures. The *Dresden Frauenkirche*, a Lutheran church, was an exception, as its decaying ruins were left untouched. After the reunification of Germany, the church was restored for $175 million.

During the firebombing of Dresden, outdoor temperatures reached as high as 2700°F, making it impossible for people to escape from their doomed homes. The military efficacy of the bombings has been questioned. Dresden was poorly defended from air attack at times, and its industries were mainly on its outskirts.

# Battle at Iwo Jima

ne of the bloodiest battles of the Pacific war ensues when 30,000 U.S. Marines storm the Japanese-held island of Iwo Jima. Americans hope to seize the island, located 660 miles south of Tokyo, to eliminate a source of interference with B-29 raids from Saipan. They also want to provide a refuge for crippled bombers on their way home from Japan.

U.S. Marines hug a sandy terrace under enemy mortar fire after landing on Iwo Jima.

A U.S. assault team warily clears a cave on Iwo Jima. The Japanese took full advantage of Iwo Jima's porous volcanic rock to burrow underground beyond the reach of U.S. heavy guns. Above ground, blockhouses with five-foot concrete walls and a multitude of pillboxes awaited U.S. Marines. These American forces had no alternative but to assault them one by one with flamethrowers and demolitions.

Private First Class Jim Michels keeps watch as Marines raise the first flag on top of Mount Suribachi. The flag was hoisted aloft on a piece of discarded pipe after a Marine patrol, led by Lieutenant Harold Schrier, had scaled the height and engaged in a brief firefight with Japanese soldiers at the summit. Later that day, another patrol brought a larger flag up the mountain. The raising of the larger flag was photographed by Joe Rosenthal and became one of the most celebrated images of World War II.

The hand of one of Iwo Jima's 21,000 Japanese defenders lies half buried in the blasted rubble. *Time* magazine correspondent Robert Sherrod observed that the dead on both sides had one thing in common: "They had died with the greatest possible violence."

# U.S. Attacks Tokyo

ate in the Pacific war, U.S. leaders realize that conventional bombing missions over Japanese cities are having only a limited effect. To rectify the problem, General Curtis LeMay implements incendiary attacks.

On February 23–24, the U.S. launches its first fire raid on Tokyo, destroying one square mile of the city. This success is followed on the night of March 9–10, when the U.S. drops 2,000 tons of incendiaries on the city. The resulting firestorm destroys 16 square miles, incinerates as many as 100,000 Japanese people, and leaves a million people homeless in the most destructive attack of the war. The heat is so intense it literally boils the water in canals.

Gnarled trees and blackened walls testify to the effectiveness of the B-29 incendiary raids on Tokyo. Though some American officers questioned the morality of the attacks, the prevailing view was that the raids were appropriate retribution for Japanese atrocities and would demonstrate to the Japanese population that further resistance was futile.

Tokyo after incendiary bomb attacks

The aircraft carrier *Hornet* supported virtually every Pacific amphibious landing from March 1944, and contributed substantially to victory in the Battle of the Philippine Sea. In February 1945, it launched air strikes on Tokyo.

# Americans Land on Okinawa

he American landing on Okinawa is the largest invasion of the Pacific war. The Navy fires more than 100,000 shells in a weeklong bombardment of the landing beaches. This expenditure is largely wasted, since Japanese general Ushijima Mitsuru has decided to fight from prepared positions inland. The initial landings by four U.S. divisions are virtually unopposed, but progress stalls when U.S. forces encounter the main defenses across the southern end of the island.

GIs of the U.S. 77th Infantry Division use spliced ladders to bridge a gulch during the fighting on Okinawa.

A flamethrower tank clears Japanese snipers from caves on Okinawa. Dug deeply into Okinawa's ridges and escarpments, the Japanese were protected from even large-caliber artillery fire while taking a heavy toll on Americans who attacked in the open. By staying in their defenses, the Japanese intended to make U.S. troops pay dearly for every foot of ground while *kamikazes* battered the ships offshore. GIs and Marines countered with tanks and small-unit assaults. The latter included flamethrowers and demolitions to eradicate subterranean enemy positions—a tactic that became known as "blowtorch and corkscrew."

A Japanese *kamikaze* pilot aims his aircraft at the USS *Missouri* in the waters off Okinawa. With the war clearly lost, the Japanese resorted to increasingly desperate measures in hopes of forcing a negotiated peace. Suicide planes sank 36 ships during the Okinawa campaign, but they could not halt the Allied juggernaut.

# The Ruhr

n March 11–12, the Royal Air Force drops almost 1,000 tons of bombs on the Ruhr—a region in western Germany vital to the country's production of coal, steel, and iron—and destroys the area's remaining road and rail bridges that provide access to the region.

On March 25, the Second British Army, Ninth U.S. Army, and First Canadian Army of Field Marshal Montgomery's 21st Army Group strike north and east of the Ruhr. In addition, General Bradley's 12th U.S. Army Group advances eastward from the south, spearheaded by General Hodges' First U.S. Army and General Patton's Third U.S. Army. The Allied advance is rapid, and—despite a concerted German attempt to break out—soldiers of the First and Ninth U.S. armies link up near Lippstadt on April 1. They thereby close the Ruhr Pocket and neutralize the thousands of German troops trapped inside it.

German soldier Hans-Georg Henke, age 15, cries after being captured by the U.S. Ninth Army in April 1945.

U.S. troops in the Ruhr Valley

The Ruhr Pocket was surrounded, along with millions of civilians and hundreds of thousands of German soldiers. During the course of the month, U.S. forces entered and seized the pocket. They found the "armory of the German Reich" reduced to ruins from Allied area bombing. The demoralized population faced years of reconstruction.

# Franklin Roosevelt Dies and Harry Truman Becomes President

Calling himself an "ordinary man," Harry Truman hailed from Lamar, Missouri. He served in World War I, prospered as a farmer, and opened a haberdashery in Kansas City. As a Democrat, he was elected judge of a county court in 1922 and U.S. senator in 1934. President Roosevelt and party leaders chose Truman as the 1944 vice presidential candidate largely because he was "safe"—not controversial.

President Franklin Delano Roosevelt dies of a stroke in Georgia on April 12, 1945. Overseas, Churchill breaks into tears when he relays the news of Roosevelt's death in a speech to the House of Commons. Stalin, reportedly, is also moved by his ally's death.

Residents of Washington, D.C., mourn the passing of President Roosevelt. Roosevelt, the only president elected four times, had pulled America out of the Great Depression and inspired his nation to victory in World War II.

When Vice President Harry Truman was summoned to the White House on April 12, 1945, he was unaware of President Roosevelt's death. When he was sworn in as president, he was not well prepared for the responsibilities of the office since, during his three months as VP, he had little contact with Roosevelt. This picture of Truman, his wife, Bess, and their daughter, Margaret, was taken as he was sworn in as president. The next day he told reporters, "When they told me what happened yesterday, I felt like the moon, the stars, and all the planets had fallen on me."

# The Fall of Berlin

 he Soviet Army encircles Berlin on April 21, 1945. German civilians fear Soviet troops, who seek retribution for the atrocities inflicted on their homes and families by the Nazis. More than 100,000 women are raped in Berlin, and thousands of Germans take their own lives in Germany, Austria, and Poland.

With 2.5 million men, the Soviets faced one million German troops, including about 45,000 male youth and elderly. The Germans were also greatly outnumbered in artillery, tanks, and planes. "The amount of equipment deployed for the Berlin operation," a Soviet soldier remarked, "was so huge I simply cannot describe it and I was there." Enormous firepower was brought to bear, but the Soviets discovered that many forward German positions had been abandoned before the bombardment. The German command pulled troops tightly around Berlin for a final, doomed defense of the city.

Stalin's troops fought through the streets of Berlin, one neighborhood at a time. Hitler ordered his Ninth and 12th armies to cut through the Soviet line and defend the city. But the Ninth was encircled and eventually decimated, and the 12th lacked the manpower and arms to attack the Soviets after holding up the Americans.

This photograph shows the aftermath of the murder-suicide of a National Socialist family in a Vienna park.

Soviet infantrymen charge past the corpse of a German soldier in house-to-house fighting for Berlin.

# Deaths of Mussolini and Hitler

n April 25, Mussolini's puppet government in northern Italy is dissolved. Two days later, Mussolini and his mistress, Clara Petacci, are captured in the Italian village of Dongo while trying to flee to Switzerland. On the 28th, Mussolini, Petacci, and 15 aides are executed.

On April 29, Adolf Hitler finally marries Eva Braun, his mistress for some 15 years. On April 30 they commit suicide together.

The bodies of Mussolini, Petacci, and four of their aides were hung by their feet while a crowd of Italians spit on and beat the remains.

FIFTEEN CENTS

MAY 7, 1945

# TIME
### THE WEEKLY NEWSMAGAZINE

"I myself and my wife…" Hitler wrote in his last will and testament on April 29, 1945, "choose death." On the 30th, the two committed suicide, Eva from biting into a cyanide capsule and Hitler from cyanide and a shot under his chin. Their bodies were carried out of the bunker, doused with gasoline, partially burned, and then buried in a shallow bomb crater.

This cover of *Time*, illustrated by Boris Artzybasheff, appeared on the issue dated May 7, 1945, a week after Hitler's suicide. When word reached America that Hitler had taken his own life, the report was met with skepticism. In fact, the FBI conducted an extensive 11-year investigation into whether the German leader faked his death. His suicide was confirmed in the 1960s by Russian journalist Lev Bezymenski.

# The Allies Liberate
# Bergen-Belsen and Dachau

n April 15, 1945, British forces enter the Bergen-Belsen concentration camp near Celle, Germany. Troops are appalled by the horrors that lay within.

During the following days, the soldiers bury 23,000 bodies on-site. Meanwhile, 29,000 of the traumatized, diseased, and starving survivors are gradually evacuated. Many inmates are treated by British medical staff. However, several thousand of those people subsequently die.

In late April, at Dachau in southern Germany, General Patton's Third U.S. Army encounters similar results of the Third Reich's barbarous policies. At Dachau, the young GIs are so incensed by what they find that they summarily execute many of the guards on-site, including members of the SS.

A truck hauls away bodies of prisoners who died at Dachau. Upon liberating Dachau on April 30, Americans discovered more than 30,000 prisoners and hundreds of unburied corpses. In its 12 years, more than 30,000 of Dachau's 200,000 prisoners died.

THIS IS THE SITE OF
THE INFAMOUS BELSEN CONCENTRATION CAMP
*Liberated by the British on 15 april 1945.*

10,000 UNBURIED DEAD WERE FOUND HERE.
ANOTHER 13,000 HAVE SINCE DIED.
ALL OF THEM VICTIMS OF THE
GERMAN NEW ORDER IN EUROPE.
AND AN EXAMPLE OF NAZI KULTUR.

"They are Jews and are dying now at the rate of three hundred a day," British soldier Peter Coombs wrote after liberating the Bergen-Belsen concentration camp. As this sign declares, the liberators discovered more than 10,000 corpses throughout the camp. British troops forced captured guards to bury the diseased bodies without the use of protective gloves.

Two women are forced to bury slave workers executed by German troops.

When Dachau was liberated, an unknown number of American GIs lined 16 SS camp guards against a coal yard wall in the adjacent SS training camp and executed them (*pictured*). Additional executions took place at Dachau's rail yard, at a guard tower, and at Würm creek. In all, 37 to 39 SS personnel were dispatched that day. These actions were "unauthorized" and did not reflect U.S. Army policy toward captured SS.

# Germany Surrenders

ictory in Europe (V-E) Day is declared as German troops continue to surrender to Allies throughout Europe.

In July 1940, the Germans easily seized and occupied the British Channel Islands. Under Hitler's orders, the islands were heavily fortified and became the sites of slave labor camps for European prisoners of war. The islands were liberated in May 1945, after Germany's surrender. Here, elated civilians on one of the Channel Islands wait to greet British troops.

New Yorkers packed Times Square on May 8, 1945, to celebrate V-E Day. By the end of the European phase of the war, the United States found itself a major player on the world stage, already assured leadership status in the soon-to-be-founded United Nations.

Here, Mrs. Pat Burgess of Palmers Green in North London waves a newspaper announcing Germany's surrender. She was one of more than a million Londoners who took to the streets to celebrate. In his speech that day, Winston Churchill somberly reminded the British that their rejoicing must be brief. "Japan, with all her treachery and greed, remains unsubdued," he said.

Field Marshal Wilhelm Keitel signs the ratified surrender terms for the German military on May 8. The terms included the unconditional surrender of all German armed forces, cessation of active operations, and surrender of all weapons and equipment to local Allied commanders. Though the document neglected to mention the civilian government, an Allied Control Council was subsequently formed with authority over all military and civilian agencies.

# Germany Suffers Consequences of War

Children play on a tank in Berlin in 1945. When not playing, they searched for food to escape hunger. "There were G.I. mess halls," remembered American private George Stone, "where at the garbage pails where you scraped off your mess kit or plate, there were small children 3–4–5 years old with a little can or pail begging for the scrapings to take home to feed the family."

To prevent black market activity, looting, and prostitution, Allied commanders made a futile attempt to prohibit soldiers from fraternizing with civilians in occupied Germany. It soon became apparent that violations of this order were unenforceable. Within six months of the fall of Berlin, more than 500,000 women turned to prostitution, many to provide for themselves and their families. Incidents of venereal disease in Berlin more than doubled in the last six months of 1945.

# Americans Secure Okinawa

A U.S. Marine takes aim with his submachine gun during an assault near Wana Ridge on Okinawa. Despite heavy casualties, the American divisions continued to batter the enemy defenses, transforming the terrain into a moonscape. Japanese resistance continued as General Ushijima Mitsuru's best units were gradually annihilated. By mid-June the Japanese 32nd Army began to collapse. Ushijima committed suicide on June 22, and Japan lost 110,00 men in the battle. American dead totaled 12,281, making Okinawa the most costly Allied operation of the Pacific war—which did not bode well for the upcoming invasion of Japan.

U.S. Marines examine an abandoned Japanese *Ohka* (Cherry Blossom) flying bomb at Okinawa's Yontan Airfield. The weapon was designed to be launched from an aircraft and guided to its target by a suicide pilot.

# Scientists Achieve the
# First Atomic Explosion

n July 16, 1945, a plutonium-core nuclear bomb is raised to the top of a 65-foot-high steel tower in the New Mexican desert. The test begins when the bomb, called "the gadget," is detonated at 5:30 A.M. It causes an explosion that is about the equivalent of 19 kilotons of TNT.

A billboard at the Oak Ridge facility demonstrates how secretive the Manhattan Project was. Located in a remote mountain area of central Tennessee, Oak Ridge served as headquarters for the entire atomic bomb project. The city never appeared on any maps, and security was enhanced by geography, fences, armed guards, and a strict system of badges and passes.

The scientists, watching 10 miles from the tower, had disagreed on what would happen following detonation—from nothing to the end of the world. The flash created by the explosion brightened the surrounding mountains and emitted a mushroom cloud about eight miles high.

# The Potsdam Conference

At the meeting, Truman told Stalin that a powerful new weapon was now ready. Having been briefed on Soviet espionage discoveries about the atomic bomb project, the president thought Stalin might already know what he was talking about. Regardless, Stalin urged Truman to use the powerful weapon promptly. Just before the meeting, Truman had been informed that the first A-bomb test conducted in New Mexico had been successful.

resident Harry Truman has his first and only meeting with Winston Churchill and Joseph Stalin in Potsdam, Germany, from July 17 to August 2, 1945. Churchill leaves before the conference ends because his party loses the British general election; he is replaced by Clement Attlee. The Potsdam agreements clarify major postwar issues for Germany and Poland. The Potsdam Declaration calls for Japan to surrender unconditionally or face complete destruction.

# Japan Surrenders Korea to the USSR and U.S.

t the urging of President Truman, the Soviet Union declares war on Japan on August 8, 1945. Included in the declaration of war is the Soviet promise of support for the independence of Korea. Soviet troops, however, enter the northern districts of the country only days later. The instrument of surrender that Japan signs on September 2, 1945, calls for Japanese troops north of the 38th parallel to surrender to the USSR, while troops to the south are to surrender to the Americans. Korea is no longer in the grip of Japan, but the nation becomes two, split north and south, Communist and free. The Korean peninsula quickly becomes a locus of grave international friction.

Residents of Seoul, Korea, greeting American troops

An American soldier chats with a female Russian officer in Korea in October 1945. Despite the outward show of friendliness, the mutual mistrust that would lead to the Cold War had already begun. Soviet troops poured into Japanese-occupied Korea well before U.S. forces were prepared to establish a presence there. U.S. leaders feared that the Russians would seize the entire peninsula and possibly move into Japan as well. An agreement was hastily reached to divide Korea in half. Much to Americans' relief, the Russians abided by the pact.

An Australian medic on New Guinea offers aid to Koreans who had been conscripted into forced labor by the Japanese. As many as five million Koreans are thought to have been taken as forced workers. How many died from 1939 to 1946 will never be known, but the estimates run as high as one million.

# The U.S. Drops the First Atomic Bomb on Hiroshima

At 8:15 A.M. on August 6, 1945, the B-29 Superfortress *Enola Gay* drops a U-235 bomb nicknamed "Little Boy" on Hiroshima, Japan. The resulting blast damages or destroys 90 percent of the city's buildings. It instantly kills upwards of 80,000 people, and thousands die later from radiation sickness.

A-bomb blast above Hiroshima

Sergeant Hugh Atkinson of Seattle was among an estimated 20 U.S. POWs killed in the atomic bomb blast at Hiroshima. However, one account indicates that Atkinson survived the bombing and was later beaten to death. The possibility exists that some of the POWs were murdered before or after the bombing. Two naval aviators who survived the initial explosion are known to have died of radiation sickness and beatings several days later.

A watch remains frozen in time, marking the exact moment the atom bomb at Hiroshima changed the world forever. In one split second, the bomb ended one era and ushered in the atomic age with all of its ramifications for politics, culture, international relations, and the continued existence of humankind itself.

Stripped of flesh by the blast, the skeleton of a Hiroshima bombing victim lies in the rubble of a house next to an unbroken ceramic pot. Many of those exposed to the fireball were simply vaporized—some leaving only their silhouettes imprinted on walls or pavement. Others died of thermal burns, from flying debris, in the collapse of buildings, or in the resulting fires.

# The U.S. Drops a Second Atomic Bomb on Nagasaki

hree days after the bombing of Hiroshima, the B-29 *Bock's Car*, carrying the plutonium bomb "Fat Man" aborts over its primary target, Kokura, due to heavy cloud cover. *Bock's Car* proceeds to Nagasaki, its secondary target, and drops the second atomic bomb of the war shortly after 11 A.M. About 25,000 people are instantly killed.

A workman stands next to "Fat Man." Unlike "Little Boy," the uranium bomb used against Hiroshima, Fat Man was an implosion-type weapon that employed plutonium. About 11 feet long and five feet in diameter, it was twice as wide as Little Boy. The new design resulted from the greater availability of plutonium and the fact that the implosion method was less susceptible to accidental detonation than the simple "gun type" ignition used with Little Boy. The new design also yielded a greater blast.

A mushroom cloud boils over Nagasaki. Heated controversy later arose over the necessity for the second bomb attack, but the mission was carried out because of the lack of reaction from the Japanese government following the Hiroshima bombing.

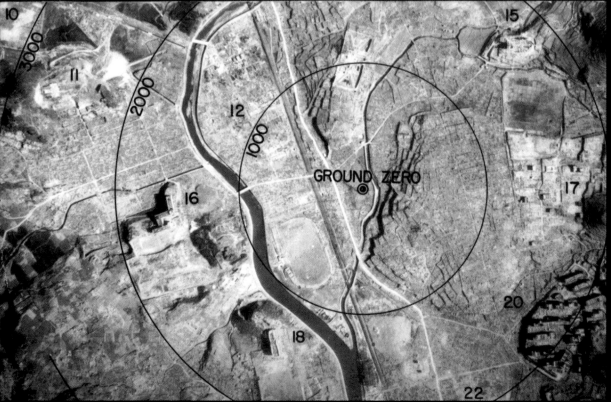

Pictured is ground zero in Nagasaki before and after the bombing. Though the city had good bomb shelters, many Japanese had become blasé about air raids and ignored the warning sirens on August 9. Due in part to the hilly topography, damage was confined to an area of about 2.3 miles by 1.9 miles. Fire was limited by waterways. Some medical services survived, and train service even continued.

# Japan Surrenders

n August 14, 1945, the Japanese news agency Domei announces that the war is over. A crowd gathers before Emperor Hirohito's palace. People weep and bow to the ground in disgrace, repeating "Forgive us, O Emperor, our efforts were not enough." Hirohito's subjects hear his voice for the first time ever the next day at noon, Tokyo time, when he formally announces the end of the war and directs the Japanese people to cooperate with the Allied occupation.

THE STARS AND STRIPES

Newspaper of U.S. Armed Forces in the European Theater

Volume 1, Number 188 — Wed., Aug. 15, 1945

# WAR ENDS

## Truman Announces
## Total Surrender

WASHINGTON, Aug. 15 (AP)—The United States, Britain, Russia and China announced today that Japan had surrendered unconditionally.

The job of disarming millions of Japanese soldiers still had to be accomplished, but it seemed that peace had returned to the world for the first time since 1937, when Japan invaded central China.

President Truman, who announced the surrender for the U.S. at 7 p. m., EWT (1. a. m., Central European Time), revealed that Gen. Douglas MacArthur had been named Supreme Commander in charge of occupation forces and would receive the surrender. Mr. Truman started his dramatic announcement by saying that he had received "full acceptance of the Potsdam Declaration, which specifies unconditional surrender of Japan." He said that arrangements had been made for the formal signing of the surrender at "the earliest possible moment."

In the meantime, he continued, the terrible atomic bomb attacks, the Superfortress raids and the fleet bombardment that had brought Japan to her knees had been ordered suspended.

The President said this note had been received from Japan through the Swiss legation:

"The Emperor is prepared to authorize and insure the signature by his government and Imperial Headquarters of the necessary terms for carrying out the provisions of the Potsdam Declaration.

"His Majesty is also prepared to issue this communication to all military, naval and air forces under their control, wherever located, to cease active resistance and to surrender their arms."

About the same time, Prime Minister Clement R. Attlee of Great Britain and representatives of the Soviet and Chinese governments—the powers that had signed the Potsdam Declaration—were announcing the surrender.

Radio Tokyo started the U.S. and the world on a celebration yesterday by announcing at 1:49 a. m., EWT (7:49 a. m., Central European Time) that "The text of an imperial message accepting the proclamation will be forthcoming soon."

At 9:50 a. m., EWT, Charles G. Ross, White House secretary, announced that the Japanese reply was "in the hands of the Swiss."

This was quickly denied by Berne. The misunderstanding seemingly arose from the receipt by the Japanese diplomats in Berne of other communications from Tokyo. The Swiss legation here issued a memorandum that "the Japanese legation reports that code cables it received this morning do not contain the answer which was awaited by the whole world." Ross then made public this memorandum without further comment.

Ross had said that when the official reply arrives here it would be delivered first to Secretary of State James F. Byrnes and then to the President.

Radio Tokyo's announcement was heard by monitors on both the East and West Coasts. But as the hours went by, it failed to read the proclamation that it had advertised would be forthcoming "momentarily."

An earlier broadcast appealed for loyalty to the Emperor, now that "the worst has come to the worst," saying:

"It is fortunate—most fortunate—that his majesty's decision on the matter is final and best. Even if the imperial command should not be in line with our individual desire, the only thing left us to do is to obey."

Doenu transmitted to occupied areas of imperial authority which explained Japanese for "the calamity caused by the U.S.," government monitors reported, but asked that it be "held for release."

*Adm. Halsey's 3rd Fleet men may be first to enter Japan*

**(Continued on Page 3)**

These reprinted front pages of Star & Stripes marked the end of hostilities in World War II. The EAA Eagle Hangar stands as a tribute to all who helped secure the peace joyously announced by these headlines. Complimentary reprints provided courtesy of the EAA Aviation Foundation and FLYING Magazine.

A Japanese prisoner of war on Guam cries as he listens to Emperor Hirohito's radio broadcast announcing Japan's surrender. Hearing the voice of their "living god" for the first time, the populace strained to make out his message through the formal language and poor reception. Millions wept. Some military officers committed suicide, while other talked of continued resistance. But for many Japanese, beneath the grief and shock was also a sense of relief. The war was over.

American newspapers splashed the news of Japan's surrender in very large type on their front pages on the 14th and 15th of August.

On August 15, more than two million people crowded into New York's Times Square anxiously awaiting word that war with Japan was over. *The New York Times* agreed to keep its revolving news sign active until the announcement was made. Finally, at 7:03 P.M. Eastern Time, a message flashed across the *Times* sign stating, "Official—Truman Announces Japanese Surrender." The pent-up energy of the revelers exploded in a whirl of hysteria. Strangers hugged and kissed each other. This picture of a sailor kissing a nurse in Times Square is not the famous photograph taken by Alfred Eisenstaedt but one taken simultaneously by Navy photographer Victor Jorgensen.

# Aftermath of War

The 1946 Academy Award for best picture went to *The Best Years of Our Lives*, which chronicled the return home of an Army Air Force officer, an infantry sergeant, and a sailor after the war. The film depicted the difficulties they and their families experienced during the readjustment.

After the surrender of Germany in May 1945, more than 11 million displaced persons (DPs), freed from slave labor and concentration camps, were now alone, hundreds of miles from home. To provide for the welfare of those remaining behind, DP camps were created throughout Germany. However, conditions of the camps were atrocious at first. "Housing conditions here [in Babenhausen] are horrible," repeated one displaced person. "They used to be stalls for the horses of the Third Reich; now they are homes for the surviving Jews."

Young children, such as this boy, sold or bartered whatever they could to survive on the streets of Berlin. Here, an orphan attempts to trade his father's Iron Cross, earned for bravery in battle, for cigarettes. A black market developed in Berlin, with cigarettes, liquor, and chocolate as three of the commodities most sought by Berliners from occupation troops.

During the winter of 1945-1946, upwards of 20 million displaced persons either lived in camps or struggled to survive in all major cities of Europe. Those pictured here were among 150 people who walked from Poland to Berlin to find food and shelter. Vital resources were lacking in those countries most affected by the war.

# The Nuremberg Trials

A total of 13 war crime trials against more than 200 persons are held in Nuremberg, Germany, from 1945–1949.

The Allies impose their judicial retribution upon Nazis who have inflicted unprecedented devastation, untold misery, and death on an industrial scale upon so many nations. It is considered poetic justice that the International Military Tribunal convenes at Nuremberg—the city that has hosted spectacular party rallies during the Nazis' consolidation of power in the 1930s.

Illustration by Kukryniksky, a trio of Russian cartoonists

The trial that received the most attention was the first, which involved 22 prominent Nazi leaders—all of whom were tried on one or more of four war-crime counts. Throughout the trial, Hermann Göring (*far left*) was a leader of the defendants, often dictating their responses to prosecution witnesses. Göring used his skills in manipulation to try to outwit the American prosecutor.

Martin Bormann, head of the Nazi *Parteikanzlei* (Chancellery), completely controlled personal access to the *Führer*. By manipulating Hitler, Bormann also affected Nazi Party directives, promotions, appointments, and finances. He disappeared after the wedding of Hitler and Eva Braun. Evidence indicates that he perished in Berlin while trying to escape through heavy gunfire. After the war, Bormann was tried at Nuremberg *in absentia*. He was convicted and sentenced to death.

Julius Streicher, pictured after his hanging, was the editor of *Der Stürmer*, the most popular anti-Semitic publication in Germany before and during the war. The June 1939 edition was a typical issue, depicting on the front page a "Jewish devil-snake" attacking a topless Aryan maiden. Streicher was one of the 22 defendants in the first Nuremberg trial—and among the 12 sentenced to death. He was the most defiant of those hanged, exclaiming "Heil Hitler" moments before his death on October 16, 1946.

# Tensions Grow between the U.S. and Russia

he Soviets and the Western powers begin strongly disagreeing on almost every postwar issue. The future of Germany cannot be settled, since neither side is prepared to see a reunited German state dominated by one of the two ideologies.

Europe is split between a capitalist west and a Communist east, divided by what Winston Churchill famously calls an "iron curtain." Over the next two years, Communist regimes are confirmed in all the states of Eastern Europe occupied by the Red Army.

In 1949, the Soviet Union tests its first atomic bomb. That same year, the U.S. helps organize a defensive pact, the North Atlantic Treaty Organization (NATO), to link the major Western states together for possible armed action against the Communist threat.

News that Russia had successfully tested an atomic bomb in September 1949 shattered any complacency in the West about the seriousness of the so-called "Soviet threat." Soviet possession of the bomb brought military parity to the ideological struggle and initiated a different form of conflict, soon to be dubbed "the Cold War."

President Harry Truman signs the North Atlantic Treaty, which marked the beginning of NATO and the end of any lingering hopes that the Soviets and the West could collaborate constructively in the postwar world.

Before the war ended, the Big Three Allied leaders signed an agreement to divide postwar Germany into four zones and Berlin into four sectors, each administered by an Allied nation, until Germany was eventually reunified. Berlin sat well within the Soviets' zone. Stalin did not agree with the other Allies' plan to rebuild Germany's economy. He therefore blocked access to the western sectors of Berlin on June 24, 1948.

Children cling to the branches of a tree near Berlin's Brandenburg Gate as a U.S. cargo plane roars overhead. The plane bears food and supplies for the city, which had been blockaded by the Soviets.

# Japan Rebuilds after War

rom 1945 to 1952, Japan comes under Allied control, with General Douglas MacArthur serving as the Supreme Commander of the Allied Powers (SCAP). His administration is small but determined to fulfill its mission of demilitarizing and democratizing Japan while establishing a viable economy.

Japan signs the Treaty of Peace with its wartime antagonists on September 8, 1951. The occupation formally ends on April 28, 1952. Firmly aligned with the West, Japan begins a long, sustained period of economic growth.

Women tend to gardens near newly built wooden barracks in Hiroshima in 1946, as the city takes the first struggling steps toward rebirth. Bomb survivors first built huts from scavenged materials. Three months later, with aid from the occupation government, construction began on wooden barracks to house the thousands of people returning to the city.

Construction site in Tokyo, 1949